Aldous Huxley:

Brave New World

Writers and Their Works

Aldous Huxley:

Brave New World

RAYCHEL HAUGRUD REIFF

With thanks to Kelly Garneau, professor of English at Northeastern University, for her expert review of the manuscript.

Marshall Cavendish Benchmark
99 White Plains Road
Tarrytown, NY 10591
www.marshallcavendish.us

Library of Congress Cataloging-in-Publication Data

Reiff, Raychel Haugrud.
Aldous Huxley: brave new world / by Raychel Haugrud Reiff.
p. cm. — (Writers and their works)
Includes bibliographical references and index.
Summary: "A biography of writer Aldous Huxley that describes his era, his major work—Brave New World—his life, and the legacy of his writing"—Provided by publisher.
ISBN 978-0-7614-4278-3
1. Huxley, Aldous, 1894-1963—Juvenile literature. 2. Huxley, Aldous, 1894–1963. Brave new world—Juvenile literature. 3. Authors, English—20th century—Biography—Juvenile literature. I. Title.
PR6015.U9Z846 2009
823'.912—dc22
2008049006

Publisher: Michelle Bisson
Art Director: Anahid Hamparian
Series Designer: Sonia Chagbatzanian

Photo research by Lindsay Aveilhe and Linda Sykes, Linda Sykes Picture Research, Hilton Head, SC

The photographs in this book are used by permission and through the courtesy of: Murray Garrett/Hulton Archive/Getty Images: cover, titlepage; ©Estate of George Platt Lynes/Conde Nast Collection/Corbis: 6; Adoc-photos/Art Resource, NY: 11; Estate of Laura Huxley: 13; National Portrait Gallery, London: 17, 22; Hulton Archive/Getty Images: 19; Topham/The Image Works: 23; © 1978 Sanford Roth/LACMA/MPTV Archive: 29; Bettmann/Corbis: 32; Wolf Suschitzky/Time Life Pictures/Getty Images: 34; The Granger Collection: 36; The Everett Collection: 43, 89; Hulton-Deutsch Collection/Corbis: 49; Elliott Erwitt/Magnum Photos: 53; Cover illustration from Aldous Huxley, *Brave New World*. Copyright 1994 Flamingo Modern Classics, an imprint of Harper Collins Publishers. Used by permission: 60; The Kobal Collection: 67; Universal TV/The Kobal Collection: 73; Cover illustration from Aldous Huxley, *The Doors of Perception and Heaven and Hell*. Copyright 2004 Perennial Modern Classics, an imprint of HarperCollins Publishers. Used by permission: 100; Michael Ochs Archive/Getty Images: 102.

Printed in Malaysia
1 3 5 6 4 2

Table of Contents

Aldous Huxley was a deeply philosophical man even in his youth, and increasingly so as he got older.

Introduction

ALDOUS HUXLEY (1894–1963) was born into a distinguished family that was well known in England in the fields of science and literature. Although he was hindered by semi-blindness, he developed his literary gifts as a novelist, short-story writer, poet, playwright, travel writer, biographer, essayist, and critic, becoming one of the most influential English writers of the mid-twentieth century. Huxley began his long writing career by publishing poetry, but he soon turned his attention to novels, making a name for himself as one of the most brilliant social satirists. After coming to America in 1937 and living through the disillusionment of World War II, he transformed himself into a deeply religious writer who made it his mission to teach others how to experience the spiritual world.

Literature was not the only interest of this multitalented, brilliant man. He was also a philosopher, mystic, social prophet, political thinker, and world traveler who had a detailed knowledge of music, medicine, science, technology, history, literature, and Eastern religions. Possessing an insatiable curiosity, he wanted to learn everything and try anything—a diet, an exercise, a philosophy, a drug. In both his public and private life, he was an unconventional free thinker. As part of his religious quest, he experimented with psychedelic drugs. His books about these experiences, *The Doors of Perception* and *Heaven and Hell*, were very influential in the drug culture of the 1960s and 1970s. Huxley was a social person, enjoying the company of his wife, son, brothers, sisters-in-law, and numerous friends—writers, scientists, mystics, actors, musicians, philosophers, and doctors. A man of good humor and wit, Huxley is best known today as the author of *Brave New World*, a novel with a vision of the future that brings out the dangers of the present.

s of the Brave New World. Not only do the inhabitants be
everyone sexually, but also they belong to one anothe
king members of the state, as their slogan "Every one w
every one else" shows. Since they all are nee
erybody's happy now," a motto that helps the citizens
tented with their shallow lives. In addition, they l
at everything that happens is good since "Ford's in
ivver. All's well with the world," words adapted from
ristian slogan, "God's in his heaven. All's well with
rld."

Identity is formed by giving sleep lessons in class
ousness, such as the one taught to Beta children: "A
ildren wear grey. They work much harder than we do, bec
ey're so frightfully clever. I'm really awfully glad
ta, because I don't work so hard. And then we are much
than the Gammas and Delta. Gammas are stupid. They
ar green, and Delta children wear khaki. Oh no, I d
nt to play with Delta children. And Epsilons are still w
ey're too stupid." "Every one belongs to every one else" i
the basic premises of the Brave New World. Not only do
habitants belong to everyone sexually, but also they be
one another as working members of the state, as their
n "Every one works for every one else" shows. Since they
e needed, "Everybody's happy now," a motto that helps the
ens feel contented with their shallow lives. In addi
ey learn that everything that happens is good since "F
his flivver. All's well with the world," words adapted
e Christian slogan, "God's in his heaven. All's well with
rld."

Identity is formed by giving sleep lessons in class
ousness, such as the one taught to Beta children: "A
ildren wear grey. They work much harder than we do, bec
ey're so frightfully clever. I'm really awfully glad
ta, because I don't work so hard. And then we are much
than the Gammas and Delta. Gammas are stupid. They
ar green, and Delta children wear khaki. Oh no, I d
nt to play with Delta children. And Epsilons are still w
ey're too stupid." "Every one belongs to every one else" i
the basic premises of the Brave New World. Not only do
habitants belong to everyone sexually, but also they be
one another as working members of the state, as their
n "Every one works for every one else" shows. Since they

Chapter 1

The Life of Aldous Huxley

ON NOVEMBER 20, 1963, two days before he died, Aldous Huxley, too weak from cancer to type or hold a pencil, was speaking into a tape recorder to finish his final work, "Shakespeare and Religion," when he uttered six words that summarized his beliefs: "Our business is to wake up!" (174). In his numerous writings and lectures, this remarkable man wanted to teach people "to wake up" so that they could live fully.

In "Shakespeare and Religion," Huxley expressed three ways in which people need to wake up. First, he said, we must realize that there is more to life than we commonly perceive by finding "ways in which to detect the whole of reality. . . . We must be continuously on our watch for ways in which we may enlarge our consciousness." Second, while we are searching for ultimate reality, we need to recognize that "we must not attempt to live outside the world, which is given to us." And third, we must "somehow learn how to transform [the world] and transfigure it" ("Shakespeare and Religion," 174). Huxley used his "multi-faceted mind" (Heard, 101) and his "fearless curiosity" (Isherwood, 157) to try to understand both the spiritual and physical worlds and to try to improve the world.

For those who did not know Huxley personally, he is best defined by his third wake-up call, to transform and transfigure the world. He was, as his brother Julian said, "a prophet" who used his "malicious wit" (Julian Huxley, 21, 23) to try to make people recognize their follies.

Therefore, many readers know him as a "disillusioned, cynical and even savage" (Osmond, 116) advocate for change who "sneers and jeers" and "cast[s] his scornful and lofty gaze on our hedonist society" (Hitchens, vii).

But he was not a savage pessimist in his personal life. In spite of recognizing world problems, he did not find life hopeless. In fact, as he aged, he became a religious man who "had a profound sense of some spiritual reality, not to be apprehended by the senses, existing beyond the confines of time and space, serene, inviolate, ineffable. . . . [T]he spiritual world was intensely real to him, irradiating his soul with 'bright shoots of everlastingness' and imbuing it with a fortitude that stood the shocks inflicted on him by fate" (Cecil, 14).

Although Huxley believed in a spiritual world, he lived intensely in the physical one, always extremely curious about scientific and technological advances and acutely aware of world events. He lived happily with others, treating everyone with love and kindness. The two words most frequently used by his friends and relatives to describe him are "gentle" and "sweet." In one of his last public speeches, he told the audience, "It is a little embarrassing that, after forty-five years of research and study, the best advice I can give to people is to be a little kinder to each other" (quoted in Laura Huxley, 117), advice he practiced daily. His widow relates that he was always loving and gentle, telling her, "one never loves enough: how can I love you more?" (Laura Huxley, 117). On his deathbed, he told her, there is "never enough of beauty. never enough of love. Never enough of life. . ." (Laura Huxley, 67).

Philosopher and historian Isaiah Berlin summed up Huxley's character: He was "a wholly civilized, good and scrupulous man, and one of the greatest imaginable distinction" (153).

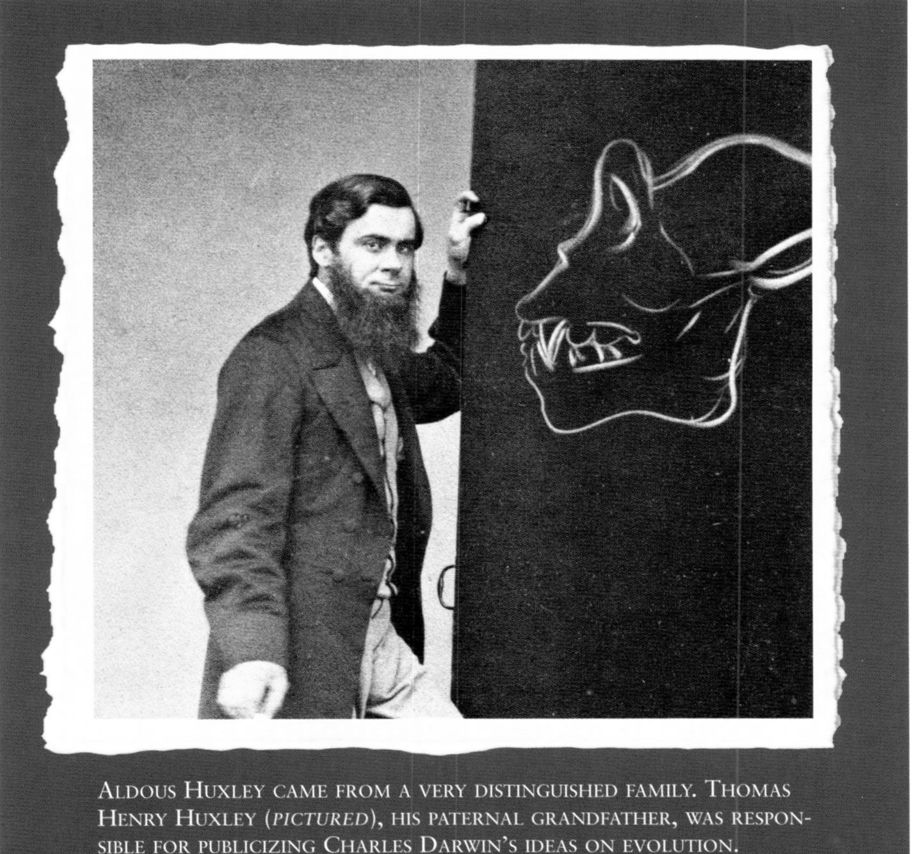

Aldous Huxley came from a very distinguished family. Thomas Henry Huxley (*pictured*), his paternal grandfather, was responsible for publicizing Charles Darwin's ideas on evolution.

Coming of Age in England

When Aldous Leonard Huxley was born on July 26, 1894, near Godalming in Surrey, England, to Julia and Leonard Huxley, he became part of two of England's most famous intellectual families. On his father's side was Huxley's grandfather, Thomas Henry Huxley, the pugnacious biologist and writer who was Charles Darwin's spokesman and brought his theory of evolution into the public sphere. Philosopher Dana Sawyer claims that "it is not hyperbole to state that Thomas Henry Huxley has had as great an influence on the course of Western civilization as either Thomas Jefferson or Thomas Edison" (15). His insistence on the benefits of science and the skepticism of religion set off a huge crisis of faith that pitted science against religion. On Huxley's mother's side were educators and writers—his great grandfather, Dr. Thomas Arnold, greatly influenced England's educational system; his great uncle, Matthew Arnold, was a literary critic and one of the most famous Victorian poets; and his aunt, Mrs. Humphry Ward, was a leading female novelist of the nineteenth century. Although overshadowed by their relatives, Huxley's parents were not ordinary people either. Leonard Huxley was an educator, editor, and publisher, while Julia Arnold Huxley founded a school for girls, a remarkable feat for this time period. With this rich heritage, Aldous Huxley looked at the world "on the one hand with the cool objectivity of a scientist and on the other with the imaginative sympathy of an artist. His Arnold side made him deeply appreciative of the past, its beauty and its wisdom. Yet he was not backward-looking. The Huxley strain in him led him to respond to the new world with intense interest and understanding" (Cecil, 13–14).

Aldous was the third Huxley son. He was close to his brothers, Julian Sorrell, age seven, who would grow up to be a famous scientist like his grandfather, and Noel Trevenen (called Trev), age five. When Aldous was five, a sister, Margaret, was born.

From a very early age, Aldous was seen as different. His brothers gave him an unusual nickname: "Ogie. Short for Ogre" (Bedford, 2), because he had a huge head, so gigantic that he could not walk until he was two because he would fall over. Julian was convinced that his little brother "possessed some innate superiority and moved on

Even as a child, Aldous Huxley spent a lot of time sitting around thinking rather than playing, as did more typical children.

a different level of being from us other children. This recognition dawned when Aldous was five and I a prep school boy of twelve: and it remained for the rest of his life. As a child, he spent a good deal of his time just sitting quietly, contemplating the strangeness of things. His godmother once saw him gazing out of the window, and asked what he was thinking about. He looked round, said the one word *Skin*, and turned his gaze out through the window again" (Julian Huxley, 21).

When Aldous was seven, his family moved two miles away from his birthplace to Prior's Field, where his mother established a girls' school. The young boy began his education here, but in the fall of 1903, when he was nine years old, he was sent to a preparatory school called Hillside. His cousin, Gervas, who was his constant companion at this time, says that although the boys were treated harshly by the schoolmaster, Aldous "possessed the key to an inviolable inner fortress of his own, into which he could and did withdraw from the trials and miseries of school existence." Unlike most of the boys at the school, Aldous was never prone to "losing his self-control or giving way to violent emotion," and, Gervas writes that,"it was impossible to quarrel with him" (Gervas Huxley, 57). It was at this school that Aldous began learning the works of Shakespeare. When he was twelve, he played the role of the merchant in *The Merchant of Venice*, performing so well that "the audience were moved to tears. Even at that age he had a singularly attractive speaking voice which lent dignity and authority to his lines, to which he also brought an extraordinary understanding and appreciation" (Gervas Huxley, 56).

In 1908, when he was fourteen, Huxley entered Eton College, an exclusive boys' school similar to an elite American high school, where he intended to study biology and become a doctor. But his plans changed after he suffered three serious blows. The first occurred a few weeks after the school year began: his mother, whom he loved dearly, died from cancer, and Huxley grieved deeply. On her deathbed, she wrote a letter to Aldous that he kept for the rest of his life: "Judge not too much and love more" (quoted in Murray, 27). Her death meant the breakup of the family. Decades later Huxley's sister described their loss: "I lost my mother, my home, my school, living in the country and my governess all at one blow" (quoted in Bedford, 25). A few months after his wife's death, Leonard Huxley moved to London, and his sons rarely spent time at his bachelor home.

The next tragedy occurred a little over two years later. In the winter of 1911, "blindness had descended on him, believed at first to be final and complete. A streptococcus had attacked and destroyed the cornea of one eye, and begun to cloud the other: for two years, he lived behind a black band, learning how to be blind" (Juliette Huxley, 42). Although the disease, diagnosed as *keratitis punctata*, forced him to withdraw from Eton, his brother says that Aldous "never complained" (Julian Huxley, 22). And he kept learning: "he taught himself to read Braille and to type on a small portable. He taught himself to play the piano—first with one hand on the Braille page and the other hand on the piano keys; then the other way round: reading with the right, learning to play with the left, until he knew both parts by heart" (Bedford, 34). He traveled to Germany to study music and learn German, and he lived in France, where he acquired an excellent French accent (Murray, 34, 36). His calm cheerfulness in the face of this tragedy is related by his cousin Gervas: "I recall going into his bedroom one very cold morning and finding him hunched up in bed with his hands under the bedclothes. 'You know, Gerry,' he said, 'there's one great advantage in Braille: you can read in bed without getting your hands cold!'" (60).

During this time his brother Trev tutored and protected him, a relationship that continued after their father remarried in 1912. Although Rosalind Bruce, the new stepmother who was younger than Julian and Trev, was kind and dedicated, she never became a mother figure to Leonard Huxley's first children.

Slowly Huxley regained some vision in his left eye, and, as a result, he was able to enroll in Balliol College at Oxford University in October 1913. With his dream of becoming a doctor shattered because of his poor eyesight, he studied English literature. The first year at Oxford was a wonderful one for Huxley. Trev, who stayed at Oxford doing postgraduate work in order to help his younger brother, was there, and Huxley made many friends. His room became the center of activity for elite young men, who were "drawn by the magnet of his mind, the curiosity of his catholic tastes, and his unassuming friendliness. Over the fireplace was pinned a picture very unlike the 'classical' reproductions generally favoured by undergraduates—a striking French poster of a group of bare-breasted nubile girls by the sea-shore. Against one wall stood a piano . . . [on which] he would strum such novelties of early jazz as 'He'd have to get under, get out or get under' or 'The Wedding Glide'" (Gervas Huxley, 60–61).

The third major tragedy occurred just before Huxley started his second year at Oxford, when his charming, loving, talented brother Trev killed himself. Biographer Nicholas Murray explains that Trev had fallen into a "serious mental breakdown" that resulted from overworking, receiving a less than excellent grade on his final college exams, failing to pass the civil-service exams, and falling in love with "a young woman who was not, according to the upper middle class codes his family lived by, 'suitable'" (37). On August 23, 1914, he hanged himself from a tree. Huxley thought Trev's suicide was an act of conscience, writing to Gervas that it "is just the highest and best in Trev—his ideals—which have driven him to his death. . . . Trev was not strong, but he had the courage to face life with ideals—and his ideals were too much for him" (Gervas Huxley, 61).

The same month Trev committed suicide, England declared war on Germany, and many of Huxley's friends joined the military. Although he was eager to serve his country, Huxley, because of his impaired eyesight, could not participate. When he returned to Oxford in October, he was lonely and isolated, but, as always, he persevered.

In 1915, during his final year at Oxford, Huxley, as critic Harold H. Watts puts it, "made an acquaintance that was both defining and practically useful to a young man who wished to enter the literary world" when he met Lady Ottoline Morrell, who "presided over a casually assembled circle of the great and the promising at her manor house in Garsington, near Oxford" (21). At the home of Philip and Lady Ottoline Morrell, Huxley became friends with the leading freethinking people of the time, including D. H. Lawrence, Bertrand Russell, Katherine Mansfield, Virginia Woolf, and T. S. Eliot.

Through Lady Ottoline Morrell, Aldous Huxley became friends with the most forward thinkers of his era in England. Here he (*left*) takes tea with (*left to right*) the Honorable Dorothy Eugénie Brett, Lady Ottoline Morrell, and her husband, Philip Edward Morrell.

After Huxley graduated from Oxford in 1916, receiving first-class honors in English literature and winning the Stanhope Historical Essay Prize, he tried to enter the army, but he was rejected as "unfit even for noncombat positions . . . because of his eyes" (Sawyer, 36). Instead he spent eight months living at Garsington, working on the farm to feel that he was doing something for the war effort. As the author of a newly published book of poems called *The Burning Wheel*, Huxley fit right in with the outspoken writers, artists, and critics. The women found him attractive: "Wearing straw-coloured jodhpurs and pale stockings, with a dark-brown corduroy jacket, he looked absent-mindedly but absurdly romantic and beautiful" (Juliette Huxley, 40).

At Garsington, Huxley met and fell in love with a young Belgian war refugee named Maria Nys, who was "small, rather plump, but lovely beyond words, with large blue-green eyes matching an Egyptian scarab ring on her long finger, a delicate slightly aquiline profile and a small pointed chin under a full mouth. Her hair, cut short, . . . hung like a dark helmet. She had the vulnerable and defenceless [*sic*] look of a child with a mature body" (Juliette Huxley, 39). Although Maria cared for Huxley, they could not afford to get married, and Maria soon left England to live with her mother and sisters in Europe.

Meanwhile, in 1917, Huxley found a temporary job as a schoolmaster at his old school, Eton. It was work he found dull, time consuming, and lonely. Some of the students, knowing of his blindness, misbehaved, reading magazines, passing notes, and gossiping, but these actions did not bother Huxley. A former student relates that although Huxley was not "a good teacher in the narrower sense of the word, . . . he was an educator in a wider sense. He showed us a glimpse of the fascination to be found in an unhampered intellectual approach to things" (Runciman, 28). One of Huxley's students was Eric Blair, who, in later life, adopted the pen name George Orwell and wrote *Nineteen Eighty-Four*.

After the war ended in 1918 and the old schoolmasters were returning to Eton, Huxley found a job in London writing for the *Athenaeum*. Now feeling

Aldous Huxley married Maria Nys in 1919 and they lived together happily—in a nontraditional marriage—until her death in 1955.

financially secure, on July 10, 1919, Huxley married Maria, whom he called "Cocola," an Italian word meaning "dear one or my darling (and a word that in its straight sense means pip or berry)" (Bedford, 87). The following year, on April 19, 1920, their son, Matthew, was born. Even though Huxley continued to work at his day job and write his own creative works, publishing three more books of poetry—*Jonah* in 1917, *The Defeat of Youth* in 1918, and *Leda* in 1920—and a book of short stories, *Limbo*, in 1920, he still needed more money to support his family. Therefore, in 1920, he took a better-paying job at *House and Garden* magazine, while also working as a drama critic for the *Westminster Gazette*. Still finding time to write creatively, he published his highly praised first novel, *Crome Yellow*, in 1921. Six months later, *Mortal Coils*, a collection of short stories, appeared, including what has become his best-known story, "The Gioconda Smile."

Living in Continental Europe and Traveling Worldwide

Huxley's work as a journalist ended in early 1923 when his publishers, Chatto and Windus, offered him a three-year contract to write two books each year, one of which needed to be a full-length novel. Delighted with this opportunity, he immediately produced a book of essays, *On the Margin*. With a steady income, Huxley was able to live wherever he wanted. For the next fourteen years, he, Maria, and Matthew made their home in Italy and France.

According to Sybille Bedford, a friend of the Huxleys, it was Maria's decision to move to Italy in order to get her husband away from a woman with whom he had fallen madly in love, Nancy Cunard. Bedford says that "Maria not only suffered from the conventional reaction—though already then she was lightly, wisely tolerant of 'infidelities'—she was disoriented: Aldous was behaving so unlike himself, and he was so unhappy." So, one night when her husband came home, she told him that she "would leave England the next morning with him or without; for him to make up his mind." Maria packed all night and "in the morning, unslept, unbreakfasted, in the clothes they stood in, Aldous and Maria left the house, drove to Victoria and caught the first train out of England. They went straight to Italy. There, in two months, Aldous wrote *Antic Hay*. He wrote it [the affair] all down, Maria said, he wrote it all out; it was over" (137–138). And that was the end of the affair that almost wrecked their marriage.

The numerous other affairs throughout their lifetimes did not threaten their marriage. Maria and Huxley had a very open relationship. In fact, when Maria knew that her husband was interested in a woman, she would help arrange for them to go to "dinner and bed" because she "thought that he enjoyed such distractions, needed the change and his mind taken off his work" (Bedford, 295). Women were easily attracted to Huxley. One female friend described him as a man of "physical beauty; he was a giant in height, with a figure that was a harmonious column for his magnificent head; the head of an angel drawn by William Blake. His faulty sight even intensified Aldous's majesty, for he appeared to be looking at things above and beyond what other people saw. But his chief trait was an intense curiosity and, while he was the greatest of all talkers, he was equally the greatest of all listeners" (Loos, 89–90).

In probably their most unusual sexual relationship, both Huxley and Maria were in love with Mary Hutchinson and carried on affairs with her simultaneously for years, even arranging for one another to spend time alone with her. In spite of these romantic interests, Maria and Huxley were devoted to one another. According to a friend, Maria, "as unusual in her way as Aldous was in his, . . . had practical virtues that made her the truest

Aldous Huxley stands with his son, Matthew, and Maria stands with an unknown boy in this photograph taken by their friend, Lady Ottoline Morrell.

helpmeet I ever knew. As well as being Aldous's best loved companion, she was his housekeeper, secretary, typist and drove his car in California. She protected him from the swarms of bores, pests, and ridiculous disciples who try to attach themselves to a great man, and all the while her unconventional reactions amused Aldous as well as amazed him" (Loos, 90).

When they moved to Italy in 1923, the Huxleys bought their first car, a four-seater Citroën, which Maria drove. Bedford says that she was "an outstanding driver, well up to professional standards, very precise, very safe, very fast. The speed was for Aldous's pleasure, the only new one, he used to say, mankind had invented since the palacolithic age" (146).

During their years in continental Europe, Huxley was busy fulfilling his contract with his publishers, in 1924 producing *Little Mexican*, a book of short stories, and in 1925 publishing the novel *Those Barren Leaves* and the essay collection *Along the Road*. But he and Maria still took time to travel widely. From 1925 to 1926, they embarked on a world tour. The work that was the result of this trip was *Jesting Pilate*, published in 1926, the same year Huxley published a book of short stories, *Two or Three Graces*, and a collection of essays, *Essays New and Old*.

When they returned to Europe, Huxley reestablished his friendship with D. H. Lawrence and his wife, Frieda. When Lawrence died in 1930, Huxley and Maria were at his side. Huxley agreed to be the editor of his letters, and *The Letters of D. H. Lawrence* appeared in 1932.

Huxley and D. H. Lawrence (*right*) were friends and intellectual soul mates.

In 1930 Huxley and Maria purchased a house in southern France on the Mediterranean coast where they lived quite simply, enjoying picnics, visits with friends, and swims in the sea. Here Huxley kept on writing, fulfilling his three-year contracts with his publishers, which were constantly renewed. He published a number of essay collections—*Proper Studies* (1927), *Do What You Will* (1929), *Vulgarity in Literature* (1930), *Music at Night* (1931), *Texts and Pretexts* (1932), and *The Olive Tree* (1936); a book of short stories, *Brief Candles* (1930); a collection of poems, *The Cicadas* (1931); a drama, *The World of Light* (1931); a travel book, *Beyond the Mexique Bay* (1934); and two well-known novels, *Point Counter Point* (1928) and his most famous work, *Brave New World* (1932). His works were extremely popular with young people such as Sir Isaiah Berlin, who hailed him as one of the "major intellectual emancipators" of the time, saying Huxley was "the object of fear and disapproval to parents and schoolmasters, the wicked nihilist whose sincere and sweetly sentimental passages—especially about music—were swallowed whole, and with delight by those young readers who supposed themselves to be indulging in one of the most dangerous and exotic vices of those iconoclastic post-war times. He was one of the great culture heroes of our youth" (144–146).

In 1933 Huxley's father died, but Huxley was not close to him and was not greatly affected by this loss.

With the possibility of another world war growing, Huxley became a leading member of the pacifist movement in 1935, advocating for peace and actively seeking to help the Jews after Hitler began his extermination program. Leonard Woolf recalled that some English men married German Jewish women so they could remain in England as British citizens; when the government tried to prevent these marriages, "Aldous and his brother Julian started a campaign against what seemed to be a barbarous abuse or misuse of authority and they mobilized all forces which might do something to prevent authority flinging the unfortunate victims to the Nazis" (35). In 1936 and 1937 Huxley published three works promoting pacifism: the novel *Eyeless in Gaza*, the pamphlet *What Are You Going to Do About It?*, and the long essay *Ends and Means*. In all of them, he preached that wars would be eliminated if people learned to get in touch with a spiritual reality through such means as meditation and yoga.

Living in America

In 1937, as things became worse on the European continent, the Huxleys decided to take an extended trip to the United States, where Huxley planned to give pacifist lectures with his friend Gerald Heard. They bought a Ford car, a choice many readers of *Brave New World* find strange since Huxley blasted Henry Ford in this novel! Once in America, they decided to settle permanently in California.

Moving to Los Angeles in 1938 was a good decision. The clean air (there was no smog around Los Angeles at that time) and bright sunshine helped forty-three-year-old Huxley see better, and the dry air was good for his delicate lungs. Maria and Huxley became part of an elite crowd, going on picnics with well-known actors such as Greta Garbo and Charlie Chaplin, and his wife, Paulette Goddard; getting to know actors Helen Hayes and Orson Welles; becoming lifelong friends with writer Christopher Isherwood and the famous scientist Edwin Hubble and his wife; and renewing friendships with the screenwriter Anita Loos, author of *Gentlemen Prefer Blondes*, and famous author Thomas Mann.

Huxley's first novel written in California was *After Many a Summer Dies the Swan*, "a parable about mortality and the vanities of wealth, based on the life of a Huxley acquaintance, William Randolph Hearst" (Sawyer, 122). Finished just before World War II began and published in 1939, this was his last novel for five years because he found it "difficult to write fiction during a war" (Sawyer, 122).

Needing to make money, he asked Anita Loos if she could help him get a job writing for the movie industry. She immediately found him work writing a movie version of *Pride and Prejudice*, a job he almost turned down. Loos wanted to know why:

> "Because it pays twenty-five hundred dollars a week," he answered in deep distress. "I simply cannot accept all that money to work in a pleasant studio while my family and friends are starving and being bombed in England."
>
> "But Aldous," I asked, "why can't you accept that twenty-five hundred and send the larger part of it to England?"
>
> There was a long silence at the other end of the line, and then Maria spoke up.
>
> "Anita," she said, "what would we ever do without you?" (Loos, 95)

Huxley did take this job and other similar ones, writing scripts for *Madame Curie*, Charlotte Brontë's *Jane Eyre*, and *Alice in Wonderland*. Much of his salary was sent to his and Maria's families back in Europe. He also continued his creative writing, publishing *Grey Eminence*, a biography of Father Joseph, an advisor to Cardinal Richelieu at the time of King Louis XIV, in 1941, and, in 1942, *The Art of Seeing*, a long essay describing and advocating the Bates method of exercising the eyes to improve vision, an unconventional method that Huxley had tried and was convinced had helped him see better.

As the war continued, Huxley's literary interests changed. According to Isaiah Berlin, "The social world about which Huxley wrote was all but destroyed by the Second World War, and the centre [*sic*] of his interests appeared to shift from the external world to the inner life of men. . . . He had a cause and he served it. The cause was to awaken his readers, scientists and laymen alike, to the connections, hitherto inadequately investigated and described, between regions artificially divided: physical and mental, sensuous and spiritual, inner and outer" (147).

Throughout the remainder of his life, Huxley made it his personal goal to wake up to the spiritual world. Not an orthodox Christian, he looked for inspiration in Eastern mysticism, studying Hinduism first with Swami Prabhavananda and later with Jiddu Krishnamurti. His reading of *The Tibetan Book of the Dead* led to his favorite novel, *Time Must Have a Stop*. Published in 1944, this book affirms the existence of an afterlife. Huxley writes, "The only hope for the world of time lies in being constantly drenched by that which lies beyond time" (quoted in Sawyer, 122).

With his new mission, Huxley was not as interested in writing novels any longer, producing only three more in the next twenty-one years before his death. He turned instead to writing a number of long, extended essays. In 1945 he published *The Perennial Philosophy*, a guide to help readers find meaning in life. In it he argues that "we are moving into darkness for lack of direct connection with the source of sweetness and light" (Sawyer, 125).

When the war ended in 1945, Huxley turned his attention to practical concerns, writing about society, politics, and economics. In his long essay published in 1946, *Science, Liberty and Peace*, he argues against the "religion of progress" by which the scientific community "deludes the public into believing that their disciplines are objective and value-free, that technological progress is the natural direction of human evolution. Whereas, in reality, when science is applied to life it is never done so, nor can it be, in a way that is value-free" (Sawyer, 133). His 1948 novel,

Ape and Essence, set in a brutal, future society in Los Angeles after an atomic war, reinforces his point that science and technology do not provide progress. Also appearing in 1948 was a screenplay adaptation of his 1922 short story, "The Gioconda Smile." Originally released as *A Woman's Vengeance* but later changed to *The Gioconda Smile*, it starred Charles Boyer and Jessica Tandy, very famous movie stars at that time.

The 1950s began poorly. First Huxley became ill with a disease that made his poor eyesight even worse. Then, in 1952, Maria was diagnosed with cancer and had a lump removed from her right breast. However, the couple was cheered by the marriage of their son to Ellen Hovde in 1950, and the birth of two grandchildren, Mark Trevenen in 1951 and Tessa in 1953.

During this decade Huxley maintained his interest in scientific and technological advances, often discussing new scientific ideas with his close friend, Edwin Hubble, the famous astronomer who demonstrated that the universe is expanding. Another friend, Robert M. Hutchins, wrote about Huxley's persistent interest in technological change: "He dragged me to Hollywood to meet a man who had a device that would slow down a phonograph to half speed and thus permit far longer and cheaper records. . . . He dragged me to lunch with the founder of the Ampex Corporation to hear the tale of building an airplane untouched by human hands that could fly to any destination with a pilot" (99–100). When Julian Huxley, a famous scientist, visited California in 1956, "[t]he brothers did the scientific sights, the new Salk Institute, . . . John Lilly's experience with dolphins, . . . the animal experiments at the University of California" (Bedford, 606). In spite of his interest in the newest scientific advances, Huxley did not always approve of them. Just as he had done in *Brave New World*, Huxley always questioned "any statement about scientific and technological

ALDOUS HUXLEY LOVED PARIS AND VISITED IT FREQUENTLY THROUGHOUT THE POSTWAR YEARS.

'progress' that omitted to take into account its effect on the quality of human life"; his friend Hutchins says he "heard him reply to a report on the wonders of modern communication, 'When we didn't communicate with Japan, we didn't go to war with her, either'" (Hutchins, 99).

In the 1950s Huxley was also looking for ways to help open his mind to spiritual reality. Therefore, he examined and experimented with a number of unconventional practices. One of these was hypnotism, which he wrote about in his 1950 book, *Themes and Variations*. Hypnotism was also a topic in his 1952 biographical work, *The Devils of Loudun*, the story of supposed demonic possession by nuns and the investigation into this matter by the Inquisition.

Besides hypnotism, Huxley, along with Maria and a group of friends who regularly met on Tuesday evenings, looked into "Scientology, animal magnetism, ESP, telekinesis, psychic prediction, séances, and other 'mumbo jumbo'" (Sawyer, 149). One of Huxley's acquaintances, music critic and conductor Robert Craft, was puzzled by this interest in such unconventional ideas, noting "the contrast between the searching, lucid, rational intelligence which was Huxley's most obvious characteristic and the most striking evidence of his Victorian inheritance, and the credulity with which he greeted (though he did not necessarily swallow whole) each new Southern Californian fad of mind and consciousness" (Murray, 389).

A major unconventional practice that fascinated Huxley was chemically induced mysticism. In 1953, when he found out that Dr. Humphry Osmond, a young doctor doing research on the psychedelic drug mescaline, was coming to Los Angeles, Huxley invited Osmond stay at his house and experiment on him. Convinced that mescaline had brought him into a higher spiritual state, Huxley wrote about his drug experience in *The Doors of Perception*, taking his title from a poem by William Blake. Although the book was a success financially, it was highly criticized. Writer Thomas Mann reacted with great hostility: "It represents the last, and I am tempted to say, the rashest development of Huxley's *escapism*, which I never liked in him. . . . Now, given the eloquent endorsement of this famous writer, many young Englishmen and especially Americans will try the experiment. For the book is selling like mad. But it is an altogether—I do not want to say immoral, but must say irresponsible book, which can only contribute to the befuddlement of the world and to its incapacity to meet the deadly serious problems of the times with intelligence" (quoted in Murray, 402). Mann was right. Numerous young men and women of the 1960s and 1970s, encouraged by one of their favorite writers and supported by people such as Harvard University professor Timothy Leary and poet Allen Ginsberg, eagerly experimented with psychedelic drugs. In 1956 Huxley followed this book with *Heaven and Hell*, another work based on his drug experiences. In all Huxley experimented with psychedelic drugs ten to twelve times (Laura Huxley, 131).

After living in the United States for years, Huxley and Maria decided that they wanted to become American citizens like their son, and in November 1953, they presented themselves for examination. When Huxley refused to bear arms for the United States and would not state that his objections were based on religious ideals, the only excuse allowed, the judge had to adjourn the proceedings. The Huxleys remained in the United States as resident aliens until their deaths.

By this time, Maria had become very sick with a recurrence of cancer. Not wanting her husband to know that she was dying, she visited Europe with him in the spring of 1954. While they were there, Huxley worked on *The Genius and the Goddess*, the last book of her husband's that Maria read. When the couple returned to California in September, Maria was very sick, but it wasn't until a few days before her death that Huxley finally realized the gravity of her illness. She died on February 12, 1955, with her husband at her side, reminding her that she was loved in this life and could go into the next life of love. As was his custom, Huxley spoke very little about the pain he felt at her death, saying simply, "It is like an amputation"

(Laura Huxley, 27). After a lonely year, Huxley married Laura Archera, his and Maria's friend, in March 1956.

In spite of his loss, Huxley continued writing. In 1956, besides publishing *Heaven and Hell*, he also published a collection of old and new essays, *Adonis and the*

AFTER HIS BELOVED MARIA DIED, HUXLEY MARRIED LAURA ARCHERA, WHO HAD BEEN FRIENDS WITH BOTH OF THEM.

Alphabet, printed in the United States as *Tomorrow and Tomorrow and Tomorrow*. Much of his time was spent working on a stage production of *The Genius and the Goddess*, which opened on Broadway in December 1957 but closed after five nights, a complete failure. In 1958 he reexamined the ideas found in his most famous novel and wrote *Brave New World Revisited*, stating that the nightmarish world he had written about in 1932 was coming about even faster than he had anticipated.

Although he enjoyed traveling around the country lecturing on college campuses on topics such as *The Human Situation* (which was published posthumously in 1977) and *What a Piece of Work Is Man*, the early 1960s were hard years for Huxley. In 1960 he was diagnosed with cancer of the tongue. The doctors recommended surgery, but he and Laura chose to have him treated with radium, and his tongue healed. Another calamity occurred in May 1961 when the Huxleys' house was destroyed by fire. All of Huxley's and Maria's letters, Maria's diaries, Huxley's manuscripts, library, and notes burned up. As always, Huxley took his loss without complaint. When Anita Loos called to express her sympathy, she said, "I could sense that he was smiling when he said quizzically, 'It was quite an experience, but it did make one feel extraordinarily *clean*'" (96–97). He wrote to his friend Robert M. Hutchins, "I am evidently intended to learn, a little in advance of the final denudation, that you can't take it with you" (Hutchins, 100).

A month later Huxley finished his last novel, *Island*. Published in 1962, the book is the story of an authentic Utopia in which people live in harmony with nature and one another, measuring progress by individual spiritual growth. He had worked on this book for years and was disappointed when a number of people reacted negatively, finding it, as Bedford says, "a boring tale of preaching goody-goodies" (712).

By June 1962 Huxley's cancer had returned, this time appearing on a gland on the side of his neck. Dr. Max Cutler removed the gland and gave him a series of cobalt treatments, enabling him to write a short, optimistic book called *Literature and Science*, which would be published in 1963. However, the cancer would not go away. Refusing to give in to the disease, in August 1963, Huxley flew to Stockholm to meet with the World Academy of Arts and Sciences and then took a trip to Italy with Laura. In his last weeks of life, Huxley was determined to complete an essay that he had promised to write, "Shakespeare and Religion," finishing it the day before he died.

HUXLEY WAS SURVIVED BY HIS BROTHER JULIAN (*LEFT*), WHO HAD MADE A NAME FOR HIMSELF AS A SCIENTIST.

On Friday, November 22, 1963, Huxley was too sick to be aware that President John F. Kennedy had been assassinated. Just before noon, the author, too weak to speak, wrote Laura a note asking for LSD, which she administered to him, convinced that he was "taking a mind-enlarging drug *in extremis*, and she saw it as a sign of his awareness and acceptance" of approaching death (Bedford, 741). She sat by his side, helping him meet death by telling him, "Light and free you let go, darling; forward and up. . . . You are going toward Maria's love with my love. You are going toward a greater love than you have ever known" (Laura Huxley, 306). The sixty-nine-year-old author died at 5:20 P.M.

Matthew, Huxley's son, was unable to come immediately because of the national chaos caused by the death of the president, but he arrived later that night. He and Laura agreed that the body should be cremated and that there would be no funeral service. On Sunday, friends and family met for tea and took a walk on the path Huxley had taken every day until he was bedridden. The following month a memorial service was held in London. In 1971 Huxley's ashes were returned to England, where they were buried in his parents' grave in Surrey after a short service. The following year a service was held for Maria, and her ashes were buried next to her husband's.

Huxley's life was a testament to his belief that "we need to wake up." With his lifelong emphasis on searching for the ultimate reality while remaining curious about everything taking place in the world, living lovingly with others, and trying to transform the world into a better place, Huxley was able to write to a correspondent shortly before he died, "I have known that sense of affectionate solidarity with the people around me and the Universe at large—also the sense of the world's fundamental All-Rightness, in spite of pain, death, and bereavement" (quoted in Laura Huxley, 312).

Aldous Huxley was born five years after the Eiffel Tower was built. In his later years as a writer, he would often sit in its shadow, sipping a drink and thinking about his writing.

Chapter 2

Huxley's Times

Years of Peace: 1894-1914

In 1894, when Aldous Huxley was born, the scientific revolution was transforming lives and ideas. One of the leading scientists of the times, Thomas Henry Huxley, Aldous's grandfather, enthusiastically described the nineteenth century as a period of "the rapid growth of the scientific spirit" with "the consequent application of scientific methods of investigation to all the problems with which the human mind is occupied" and the "rejection of traditional beliefs which have proved their incompetence" (quoted in Day, 13). Huxley was raised to believe in his grandfather's optimistic view of scientific progress, an outlook he dismissed when he became an adult.

As a child, Huxley saw the evidence of the scientific revolution all around him. He was born five years after the Eiffel Tower, the "world's tallest structure and a symbol of confidence in science and technology," was erected (Sawyer, 40). New inventions were making people's lives more enjoyable. Just a few years before his birth, scientists had invented the telephone (1876), the combustion engine (1885), and the light bulb (1879). When Huxley was a little boy, Guglielmo Marconi came out with the wireless telegraph (1896) and Kodak introduced the "Brownie" camera with removable film (1900). Exciting new explorations were occurring; of particular interest in England was Captain Robert Scott's first expedition to the Antarctic from 1900 to 1904 (Fraser, 626). Transportation was becoming faster and easier. Henry Ford introduced the first automobile in 1896, and public transportation also improved. By the early twentieth century, London was "full of motor buses" and several were "sunk deep underground, making travel round London much faster" (Fraser, 626). In 1903, when Huxley was nine, the Wright brothers made the first airplane flight. All of these developments led many people to believe in the idea of world progress.

Promoting the ideas of change and progression were a group of left-leaning intellectuals who were known as the Bloomsbury Group, a "handful of gifted publishers, writers, artists and art historians" (Fraser, 626), people with whom Huxley lived at Garsington during World War I. These intellectuals especially venerated Sigmund Freud, who published his first book on psychoanalysis in 1895 when Huxley was one year old. Huxley's friend, D. H. Lawrence, was drawn to Freud's idea that instinct was more important than the intellect (Fraser, 626), but Huxley was "never an admirer of Freud" (Murray, 435).

One way progressives tried to make the world a better place was to promote fairness in British life. Humanitarians, feeling that the state had an obligation to care for the sick and the elderly, passed legislation for old-age pensions in 1908 and national insurance in 1911 (Fraser, 632). Progressives believed that the British colonies would soon be independent, since the British Empire was "merely a trustee for the future. Britain's role was to guide them to democracy when they were ready" (Fraser, 630). Optimistic Europeans worked for universal peace because war was now "out of fashion and seemed uncivilized; it belonged to a less advanced age" (Fraser, 625). Although the first international discussion of armaments and warfare was held at The Hague, Netherlands, in 1899, and a second one took place in 1907, there was little or no progress made in disarmament.

People viewed the world as getting better, noting that governments were able to change rulers peacefully. During

Huxley's early life, Great Britain was ruled by three different monarchs, and each accession was carried out in an orderly fashion. Queen Victoria died in 1901, leaving the crown to her son, Edward VII. When he died in May 1910, fifteen-year-old Huxley lined the route of his funeral as a member of Eton's Officers' Training Corp (Murray, 30). George V then became king, ruling until 1936.

In spite of the general optimism, things were far from perfect. In Great Britain, unions and suffragists who were dissatisfied with government reforms staged a series of strikes from 1911 to 1914. In Europe, tensions were mounting between nations because of political and economic competition. The breaking point came on June 28, 1914, when Archduke Francis Ferdinand, heir to the Austro-Hungarian Empire, was assassinated by a Bosnian Serb. Germany encouraged the Austrians to crush the Serbs, marking the beginning of World War I (Fraser, 652). Huxley and his young friends, however, paid little attention to politics and world affairs. Writing in later life, Gervas said, "Looking back it seems extraordinary that we should have shown such a complete lack of concern with the current issues that were so deeply affecting our country and the world" (quoted in Murray, 43).

World War I: 1914-1918

Huxley was twenty years old on August 4, 1914, when Great Britain declared war on the Central Powers, composed of Germany, Austria-Hungary, and Turkey, after the Germans invaded Belgium on their way to attack Britain's ally, France. Although Huxley at first wanted to join the war effort, he soon became antiwar like his Garsington friends, who were "uniformly opposed to the war" (Sawyer, 38). He became violently opposed when Maria Nys was trapped on the continent because of the raging war, separating the young lovers for two years. By 1917, Huxley regarded the war as becoming "more ghastly every day . . I think that it is folly and a crime to go on now" (Bedford, 83).

The United States entered the war in 1917, the same year that Russia, another ally of Great Britain, withdrew its support of the war when the Bolshevik Revolution began. Russia's leader, Vladimir Lenin, urged the starving Russian soldiers to desert and return home. Even though Russia was gone, the other Allies did not give up until they defeated the Central Powers on November 11, 1918. The Treaty of Versailles, which "economically speaking," Huxley felt "was a thoroughly bad peace" (Bedford, 330), officially marked the end of the war. It treated the Germans harshly, making them bitter and eager for revenge.

During the war years, writers reflected bleak feelings of despair, as seen in such works as *Dubliners* (1914) and *Portrait of the Artist as a Young Man* (1916) by James Joyce, a very famous writer Huxley did not admire, although he admitted in 1938 that "even his unintelligible things read musically" (Murray, 315), and *Prufrock and Other Observations* (1917) by T. S. Eliot, a friend whom Huxley thought "didn't know nearly as much as he pretended, with his literary allusions and his pompously serious essays" (Murray, 315).

In spite of the unsettling times, Huxley enjoyed a new innovation coming from America, the cinema. "He saw the film version of *Jane Eyre* after which he said he wanted to see *Birth of a Nation* [an influential but racist American movie that became Hitler's favorite film] which was 'said to mark a new epoch in cinematographic art'" (Murray, 61).

World War I "changed fundamentally the ways in which people thought and wrote" (Peck and Coyle, 224). Whereas before 1914, intellectuals such as Huxley were "confident that human beings were rationally inclined and needed only a bit of clear-sighted direction to construct the better world" (Day, 268), by 1918, they had lost their "traditional structure of values, understanding and reassurance" (Peck and Coyle, 228).

The 1920s

Huxley was not optimistic when the war ended. He not only recognized that Great Britain had lost hundreds of thousands of young men, but he also realized that its economy was ruined, making it very difficult for him to find work at a living wage. During the war, "prices more than doubled, taxation reached about five times the prewar levels, and the burden of domestic and foreign debt increased 10 times between 1914 and 1918" (Day, 266). The situation became worse in the following decade as laborers went on strike to protest poor wages and the lack of jobs. In the early 1920s Huxley struggled to make enough money to support his wife and infant son, working multiple jobs to make ends meet.

Besides economic problems, the British also faced political troubles with Ireland. In 1921 Southern Ireland, which was Roman Catholic, became an independent nation called the Irish Free State, while Northern Ireland, which was Protestant, remained part of the United Kingdom. On the continent, the Soviet Union was established in 1922, the same year a Fascist government led by Benito Mussolini was put into place in Italy. At this time, the Huxleys were not very concerned with the Fascists, seeing them "rather as comic opera buffoons than as the stormtroopers of a sinister ideology" (Murray, 151). In fact, the Huxleys moved to Italy in 1923. However, in 1925, "it was brought home to Aldous and Maria that they were living in Fascist Italy. Four ruffians in uniform forced their way into [their house] and demanded to search the place," causing Huxley to view the Fascist regime as "wicked, stupid and fantastically incompetent," a government that was "worse, yes a good deal worse, than a democracy, say, such as France or England (with their bitter inequalities and hypocrisies)"; however, he saw both types of government as "part of the general inhumanity and folly" (Bedford, 159–160).

In spite of economic and political troubles after the war, new technological and scientific developments made life better for many people. Henry Ford's assembly-line process, which he put in place in 1913, produced affordable cars, making it possible for Huxley and Maria to buy their first car when they moved to Italy. Airplanes also improved, and in 1927 Charles Lindbergh flew solo across the Atlantic. Other scientific advances also contributed to people's well-being. Millions of families had new household appliances, such as electric refrigerators, electric washing machines, and vacuum cleaners (Freidel, 260). People were entertained by radios in their homes, and they had quick access to just about any person by telephone. Chemists, biologists, and bacteriologists improved public health and lengthened the average life span (Dulles, 348–349).

Younger people and the intellectual elites rebelled against old ways of thinking, and they embraced relaxed moral codes. This was the way of life that Huxley and the Garsington crowd practiced, believing that "sexual freedom of action was a prerequisite of being civilized" (Bedford, 95). Writers shared the disillusionment of the times. Huxley, who expressed the "profound cynicism" of the age in *Crome Yellow* (1921) and *Antic Hay* (1923), was looked upon as a type of "prophet, an 'intellectual emancipator,' who challenged traditional values and pointed up their dissatisfaction with hollow posturing and moral hypocrisy. He became a hero, an articulate voice for what Gertrude Stein called the 'lost generation'" (Sawyer, 47–48). Huxley's Garsington friends, Virginia Woolf, T. S. Eliot, and D. H. Lawrence, as well as other writers such as E. M. Forster, Ezra Pound, James Joyce, and William Butler Yeats, also articulated the pessimistic mood that had begun with World War I.

While writers were reflecting the cynicism of the times, musicians were discarding old styles of music. In the 1920s many young people began listening to jazz, the music that started with black musicians in New Orleans and quickly spread throughout the United States and then to England. It was made popular by "Jelly Roll" Morton, Louis Armstrong, and Aaron Copland (Freidel, 266–272). Years earlier Huxley had enthusiastically played jazz as an Oxford student, but now he "whole-heartedly" loathed

THOUGH HUXLEY HATED "TALKIES," THE MOVIE *THE JAZZ SINGER* USHERED IN A POPULAR ART FORM THAT HAS LASTED INTO THE TWENTY-FIRST CENTURY.

this type of music (Bedford, 44). Listening to a jazz band in 1929, he found "its melodies and sentimental lyrics" signs of "corruption" (Murray, 228). Movie theaters were packed in the 1920s, as crowds watched silent films with stars such as comedian Charlie Chaplin. They became even more popular with the introduction of talking films in 1927 (Freidel, 260; Dulles, 346–347), an innovation Huxley hated from the time he saw his first talkie in 1929, *The Jazz Singer,* which he described as "the latest and most frightful creation-saving device . . . of standardized amusement" (Murray, 228). Two years later, he lamented that England had adopted these vulgar forms of entertainment, saying, "I can make nothing of it; the harsh music, the blatant vulgarity, the Talkies" (Murray, 245). (Ironically, later in life, after he recognized the great financial benefits of movie-making, Huxley became a screenwriter for the Hollywood movie industry and worked to have his own writings made into movies.)

As the decade drew to a close, the good times for most people came to a sudden end with the stock-market crash in America in October 1929. However, the Huxleys did not seem to be affected, taking a two-month trip to Spain in October and November.

The Great Depression of the 1930s

After the crash, the world's economy suffered as factories and stores closed, unemployment rose, and people lost their life savings. For more than ten years, the world endured the Great Depression. However, not everyone was affected by the poor economy, including Huxley, since his income came from the sale of his books, and he was a prolific and popular writer. Therefore, while much of the world suffered, he was able to buy a home in Sanary, France, in 1930 and also rent a flat in England in 1934 so his family could live part of the year in each country. Furthermore, he and Maria had plenty of money to travel widely from 1930 to 1937, visiting London, Paris,

Belgium, Germany, the West Indies, Guatemala, Mexico, Spain, Holland, and the United States.

During this decade, the British were primarily focusing on internal affairs, concerned with the economy and also the monarchy. King George V died in 1936, leaving the throne to his oldest son, Edward VIII, who wanted to marry an American divorcée, Mrs. Wallis Warfield Simpson. When the British government, the Church of England, and many British citizens objected, Edward gave up the throne to marry her, and his brother became King George VI.

Since politicians in Great Britain and throughout the world were concentrating on their countries' economies, few leaders recognized the danger of the rise of Adolf Hitler and his Nazi Party in Germany. In 1933, Hitler, Germany's new chancellor, was determined "to destroy the humiliation of Versailles and to reclaim the land removed from Germany" (Fraser, 691). He made the Jews his scapegoats, taking away their civil liberties and enacting racist laws forbidding marriages between Jews and non-Jews (Fraser, 691). Other European countries also failed to recognize the dangers Italy posed when it became aggressive. Neither Britain nor France, the two leading powers, wanted to alienate Italy's leader, Mussolini, so when he insisted that he be given two-thirds of Ethiopia in late 1935, they agreed to his demands.

Although in 1932 Huxley looked upon Germany "with a kind of aloof voyeurism" (Bedford, 255), by 1933, after Hitler's rise to power, Huxley was not oblivious to the world situation. He was disturbed that "in Hitler's Germany the Jews are being treated as though they belonged to some species of lower animals" (quoted in Murray, 273) because he was convinced that "theories of racial superiority such as those now prevalent in fascist Europe were nonsense and the idea of racial purity a chimera . . . [since] 'any given population is a vast roulette table'" (Murray, 270). He was dismayed that military force was imminent. Wanting to secure international peace, in 1933, he proposed that an official World Psychological Conference be held to find ways to keep people "contented and in health" so they wouldn't find war justifiable (Bedford, 301). When the conference did not occur, Huxley became increasingly disturbed. He felt that "society wasn't progressing" but was instead "degenerating into a series of mob mentalities (fascism in Italy and Germany, and communism in the Soviet Union) that offered the individual a kind of solace but at too great a price. It gave them freedom from choosing rather than the freedom to choose" by "empowering tyrants like Hitler, Mussolini and Stalin" (Sawyer, 99). As Hitler gained greater power and war seemed more likely, Huxley became more worried. In the fall of 1935, he joined the Peace Pledge Union (PPU), believing that his idea of teaching individuals to do spiritual meditations would ensure lasting peace.

By this time, many of the members of the PPU had changed their pacifist attitudes because they realized that the Fascist governments needed to be stopped. In particular, they abhorred Hitler, who became empowered after he saw how England and France had appeased Mussolini, and declared in 1936 that he would no longer obey the Versailles agreement. Many members of the PPU now felt that peace was not possible. When Huxley's pamphlet *What Are You Going to Do About It?* was published in 1937, Virginia Woolf's husband "argued against its blind idealism," and Cecil Day Lewis, in his article 'We're Not Going to Do NOTHING' for *The Left Review*, said that England was not yet at the point where there was no recourse but to "while away the time with Mr. Huxley's 'spiritual exercises'" (Sawyer, 100). Huxley was not deterred; he began writing a full-length novel and arranged a lecture tour in the United States to support peace, which he began in 1937.

That same year, Neville Chamberlain became prime minister of England. Although Hitler's aggression was obvious, Chamberlain thought he could handle the German leader and avoid war. Therefore, in 1938, after Hitler seized Austria, neither Chamberlain nor the French premier did anything. When Hitler demanded part of Czechoslovakia, they agreed to let him have it, believing that Hitler would not claim any more land. Chamberlain naïvely told the British there would be "peace in our time" (Day, 266).

In this decade of failing economies and rising dictatorial leaders, Huxley, whose *Brave New World* was the most popular novel in England of the 1930s, and many other writers expressed their concerns with contemporary political and social issues. These included the leading poets of the day, W. H. Auden, Ezra Pound, and T. S. Eliot; playwright Noël Coward, whose plays Huxley admitted were "strangely successful" even though they were whipped up "like a soufflé in a vacuum" (Murray, 315); and novelist J. R. R. Tolkien. As countries struggled with the Great Depression and as dictators became more aggressive, Huxley watched as a number of intellectuals searched for order and meaning in life. Some, like the American novelist John Steinbeck, who wrote *The Grapes of Wrath*, turned to Communism as a way to solve social ills. Others, such as Eliot, turned traditional, going back to Western culture and Christianity. Huxley himself believed that the "cure for social problems is actually the improvement of the individual citizen" (Sawyer, 95), an idea he promoted in his pacifist works.

World War II: 1939-1945

In 1939 Germany began to annex smaller European countries. On September 1, it invaded Poland. The British and French warned Hitler to retreat, but when nothing happened, they declared war on Germany on September 3. World War II had begun.

The six years of war were very upsetting to Huxley, so disturbing that "of the war, six thousand miles away, he would not speak at all. Not during the first bad years." Instead he suffered silently, aware "of great present suffering that must be followed by yet more suffering. The sense of waste and folly. The sense of utter horror. Physical and moral. Unalleviated by any sense of right. For Aldous never changed the conviction he had arrived at: that war, in *any* cause, in *any* circumstances, must always by its own nature be evil and lead to further evil" (Bedford, 385).

In June 1940, France fell to Hitler's powerful forces. One of Huxley's friends recalled that on the day Paris fell, Huxley's "face was dead white, [and] he bore the expression of someone who was peering into hell" (Loos, 94). After defeating France, the Nazis turned their attention to conquering Britain. They began by bombing London, where "thousands of civilians perished, and much of central London was destroyed" (Day, 266). But the British refused to be beaten. They alone fought against Germany until the war became a worldwide conflict in 1941, when the Soviet Union joined the Allies after being invaded by Germany and when the United States declared war after the Japanese attacked Pearl Harbor on December 7.

Angry at the unjust attack, the Americans committed themselves to the war effort. Sixteen million American men and women served in the armed forces, many of them volunteering for duty. To start a western assault on the Nazis, the American and British forces landed in Normandy, France, on D-day, June 6, 1944. The fierce battle for the rest of Normandy raged throughout the summer, made worse by terrain that was interwoven with hedgerows and deep ditches where Germans waited in ambush. In spite of great losses, the Allied troops liberated Paris on August 25. From there, they swept through France, Belgium, and The Netherlands, driving the Germans back. Germany surrendered on May 7, 1945.

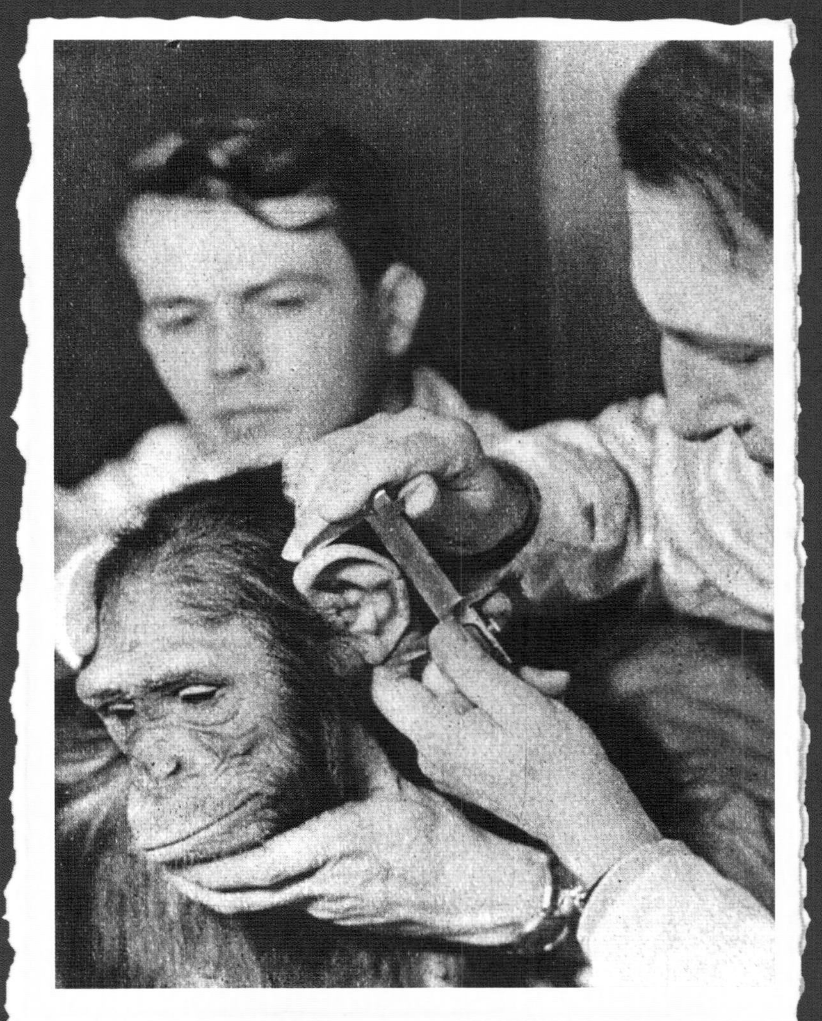

THE NAZIS WERE RESPONSIBLE FOR PREVIOUSLY UNHEARD-OF ATROCITIES. HERE, NAZI OFFICIALS USE CALIPERS TO MEASURE A MONKEY'S EAR TO HELP THEM DEVELOP A SYSTEM OF FACIAL MEASUREMENT THAT WOULD ALLOW THEM TO MEASURE RACIAL DESCENT AND DECIDE WHETHER A GIVEN PERSON COUNTED AS "HUMAN" ENOUGH TO LIVE OR LOWLY ENOUGH TO EXTERMINATE.

Several months later, after atomic bombs destroyed Hiroshima and Nagasaki, Japan also surrendered in August, and World War II was over.

While the war raged in Europe, Americans at home worked hard to help win the war. Factories were converted into plants for war supplies, and with the men away fighting, thousands of women began working in factories. Money was tight, and people willingly made sacrifices. For the Huxleys, many of the war years were lean times even though Huxley was making money writing screenplays for Hollywood; he and Maria gave away much of his earnings to help their European relatives who, Huxley wrote, were "involved in the nightmare of Europe" (Murray, 324). They sent food, arranged for family members to join them in California, donated gifts for charity auctions, and spent money to rescue two German Jewish children (Bedford, 384). After the war was over, Huxley spoke up about the horrors of the war. In 1948, in *Ape and Essence*, he blasted scientists, politicians, generals, journalists, and the common man who had allowed World War II to occur, an event that caused "the destruction overnight of a century's accumulation of wealth and all the potentialities of future prosperity, decency, freedom and culture" (129).

In spite of the devastation of the war and the creation of the atomic bomb, there were some positive outcomes of the war due to science. People in aviation designed new or improved jet airplanes, helicopters, radar, and guided missiles. Technicians worked on providing food for soldiers, which led to precooked frozen foods that became available to all consumers after the war. Scientists researched drugs, trying to find ways to help the wounded and to save lives, resulting in the wonder drugs sulfapyradine and penicillin, and other antibiotics that controlled tuberculosis, kidney infections, and other diseases (Davis and Lunger, 6–7).

Not very much literature of lasting merit was published during the war, although classics like *Oklahoma!*, by Richard Rodgers and Oscar Hammerstein, and *The Glass Menagerie*, by Tennessee Williams, appeared on stage (Snowman, 113). Movies also flourished. In a strange turn of events, Huxley, who for two decades had railed against the cinema, now was actively trying to become a part of the movie world, hoping to make "tons of money in the films" (Bedford, 350).

Postwar Years: 1945-1963

The decades after the war were marked with tension, and Huxley was "gloomy about the world outlook," often signing his letters with "exclamations such as 'What a world!'" (Murray, 382–383). Although the United Nations was founded on October 24, 1945, to help provide world security, the opposing political ideologies of democracy and communism struggled for supremacy. The United States and the Soviet Union, the two new superpowers that had fought on the same side during World War II, became bitter enemies following the war. The Soviet Union, a totalitarian state opposed to democracy, helped Communists seize control of China and most of the countries in Eastern Europe, while the United States, the world's greatest democracy, became the defender of non-Communist nations that were threatened by the Communists. The struggle between the American-led democracy and the Communist nations became known as the Cold War.

As the Cold War escalated, the two superpowers began to threaten the use of force, engaged in propaganda, and aided weak nations. Hostilities broke into fighting in 1950 when Communist North Korea, backed by the Soviet Union, invaded South Korea, which was supported by America and Great Britain. This was the beginning of the Korean War, which lasted until 1953.

The superpowers also built nuclear weapons, including the hydrogen bomb, authorized by U.S. president Harry S. Truman in 1950, and participated in a missile development race. Huxley found the nuclear arms race abhorrent. He was appalled that "the human race was determined to destroy itself" (Bedford, 514). In 1952, when he visited a U.S. naval research station whose entire purpose was "the production of bigger and better rockets" (Bedford, 514), his belief that scientists were "wretched slaves" whose scientific acts were an "orgy of criminal imbecility," which they called "Progress and Nationalism," but which were really "lunatic dreams" (*Ape and Essence*, 124, 125, 130), was reaffirmed. He described the research station as "the most frightening exhibition of scientific and highly organized insanity I have ever seen" (Bedford, 514). That same year, he published *The Devils of Loudun*, "an historical example of the diabolic possession he seemed to detect in the geopolitical world of the 1950s" (Murray, 384).

While the superpowers fought, Americans' fears of Communism were made worse by a witch hunt led by Senator Joseph McCarthy, who was determined to locate and eliminate suspected Communists who lived in the country. This movement to weed out enemies to America became known by the term *McCarthyism* in early 1950. With extravagant, unsubstantiated accusations, McCarthy, along with "a broad coalition of politicians, bureaucrats, and other anticommunist activists hounded an entire generation of radicals and their associates, destroying lives, careers, and all the institutions that offered a left-wing alternative to mainstream politics and culture" (Schrecker, xii). Huxley was on the FBI's list of suspected Communists. In 1951 the House Committee on Un-American Activities learned that Huxley was part of an organization called "Friends of Intellectual Freedom," whose purpose, according to FBI notes, was "to raise

Huxley was on the list of supposed Communists who were "red-baited" by Senator Joseph McCarthy and other people who believed that the Communists and those who shared even some of their beliefs were out to destroy American democracy.

funds to help former Communist writers rehabilitate themselves" (Murray, 398). Huxley's activities were monitored for the next two years by the Los Angeles Field Office, which cleared Huxley of Communist activities in 1953; however, the FBI kept a file on Huxley throughout the rest of his life (Murray, 306).

In spite of the fears of Communism and war, the Huxleys, like most Americans, were living in prosperity after World War II. The U.S. economy was thriving due to flourishing factories and businesses, although Huxley was "perplexed at the passion for consumer goods, cars, material possessions that gripped 1950s America" (Murray, 387). The nation's wealth was enjoyed by more and more people, as labor unions gained high wages and good benefits for their members. Many of the young adults who had grown up during the Depression and had participated in World War II were now ready to live "the good life." They started families, producing a generation of babies that would later be known as the Baby Boomers, and they built nice homes on the fringes of the cities, starting suburban living.

With more money, the Huxleys were once again able to travel, taking their first trip out of California in 1947. In the next years, Huxley and Maria took several trips to New York and also went abroad to Paris, Rome, London, and Athens. Later, Huxley and Laura also traveled widely, visiting various places in the United States, as well as going abroad to Italy, Peru, Brazil, England, France, Hawaii, Switzerland, Denmark, Belgium, Japan, India, and Sweden.

The scientific discoveries during the postwar years helped make lives better or, at least, more interesting. New ideas led to the creation of television, which became a fixture in many American and European homes. No longer were people spending most of their leisure hours reading, going to movies, or listening to the radio. Now they clicked on the TV, and became, as Huxley contemptuously called them in *Island*, "the motorized television addicts of America and Europe" (246). Huxley himself did not own a TV set, telling UCLA students in 1959 that television is "a sort of Moloch [an idol with a raging fire in which worshipers throw living people] which demands incessant human sacrifice" (Murray, 432). Outdoor drive-in theaters also became a popular attraction for families with young children and for teenagers on dates.

Medical advances helped people live longer and with fewer debilitating diseases. One new medical advance was the development of the field of psychoanalysis, which became a tool to help people with emotional problems. In 1948 Huxley and Maria both tried using psychoanalysis under the guidance of Laura Archera, who would become Huxley's second wife. Although the process did not work for them, many people, particularly those with mental illnesses, were helped by this technique. Huxley became an expert in this field, lecturing on psychology for the Menninger Foundation, a primary center of psychiatric training, in 1960. Another huge breakthrough was a vaccine for poliomyelitis. In 1953 Jonas Salk began his trial vaccine. Found effective, it became the chief weapon against this crippling disease in 1955.

Times were exciting as new technology created the *Concorde* airplane, which was able to fly faster than the speed of sound. Space exploration became a reality: satellites were placed in space in the late 1950s and in 1961, Russian Yuri Gagarin and American Alan B. Shepard Jr. became the first two people to travel in space. Huxley was not in favor of the space program. When he visited an aeronautical plant in Los Angeles in 1962 to look at the newest moon-rocket, he censured the scientists, telling them that "in all probability, the astronauts would bring back with them from the moon some virus which would wipe out everybody in the world," and he asked them "why they wanted to waste money trying to get to the moon instead of doing something about the approaching population explosion, here at home" (Isherwood, 161). He showed his disdain for the space program in *Island*, in which his ideal people feel no desire to land on the moon but instead have "only the modest ambition to live as fully human beings in harmony with the rest of life on this island" (246).

While these advances were taking place, hostilities between Communist and democratic countries continued in the 1960s. The Vietnam War, which began in 1957 as Communists and non-Communists struggled to control South Vietnam, was being fought. In 1961 the world situation was so volatile that President John F. Kennedy urged Americans to build fallout shelters in case of atomic wars. Huxley was not a fan of this popular president, "in part because of the 'distasteful' presence of old Joe Kennedy [President Kennedy's father] and his millions 'lurking in the background of the young crusader'" (Murray, 436).

Atomic war was barely averted the following year when the United States discovered that there were Soviet-built missile bases in Fidel Castro's Cuba, an island located only ninety miles from the American mainland. On October 22, 1962, President Kennedy ordered a blockade to stop the Soviet ships from delivering any further shipments of arms. Nuclear war was avoided, and the crisis ended when the Soviet ships turned around. Although Huxley did not comment on this event, he maintained his loathing of militaries and nuclear arms until his death. In *Island*, Huxley described Utopia as a place where people do not want to have armies or produce armaments.

Because of world tensions, many people became rebellious and idealistic, believing they could change the world. The 1960s were progressive times, the "heyday of ideas and idealism" (Fraser, 744). The hippies, youth protesters who objected to the customs and traditions of society, were leaders in this progressive movement. Although Huxley, now in his late sixties, was not a hippie, he shared many of their ideas. The hippies, like Huxley, advocated universal love and peace. They expressed their views, in part, by protesting the Vietnam War after hundreds of thousands of American troops were drafted to fight. Bitterly opposed to this war, they staged antiwar demonstrations, making the war extremely unpopular in America.

The hippies, like Huxley, also experimented with hallucinogenic drugs. After reading Huxley's *The Doors of Perception*, young people were inspired to use marijuana and LSD freely, and thus, "Huxley unwittingly set in motion an international movement of drug experimentation involving millions of American and European youths; not accidentally did Timothy Leary and Richard Alpert later dedicate their adaptation of the *Bardo Thodol*, *The Psychedelic Experience*, to Aldous Huxley" (Dunaway, 327).

The hippies, like Huxley, wanted a just world and, therefore, they supported the civil rights movement, the main domestic social issue of the 1960s. African Americans, under the leadership of Dr. Martin Luther King Jr., staged demonstrations to make their plight known to the American people. A year after Huxley's death, the Civil Rights Act was passed. This act legally eliminated discrimination in employment, voter registration, and public housing. Besides African Americans, other disenfranchised people, such as American Indians and Mexican Americans, also began to advocate for more rights.

Like the hippies, many literary artists were disillusioned with life and rebelled against established society, writing about lonely, disillusioned people who suffered because of corrupt societies. The antihero—a failure, a rebel, or a victim—became standard in American fiction, beginning with Arthur Miller's *Death of a Salesman* in 1949, a work Huxley did not like (Murray, 395). In 1951 J. D. Salinger's bestseller, *The Catcher in the Rye*, portrayed the dilemma of a young nonconformist hero longing for a meaningful life. The following decade, Sylvia Plath's *The Bell Jar* related the story of a vulnerable girl trapped because of society's expectations of conformity. Many Jewish-American writers—including Saul Bellow, Bernard Malamud, and Philip Roth—wrote about Jewish heroes who did not fit into American society. Black writers, such as Ralph Ellison and James Baldwin, reflected on the plight of black Americans. Southern short-story writers, including Eudora Welty, Flannery O'Connor, and Carson McCullers, examined changes in the South. Other popular writers, such as Norman Mailer and John Updike, looked at lonely, disappointed Americans. Allen Ginsberg's "beat" poetry and Jack Kerouac's "beat" novels, which were very popular with the hippies, were pleas for the individual to rise up against conformity.

Many British writers were also antiestablishment. For example, novelist Doris Lessing wrote about the isolated individual who could never find satisfaction in life, while novelist Kingsley Amis satirized contemporary British society; dramatist Tom Stoppard, in *Rosencrantz and Guildenstern Are Dead*, focused "on little men in a world beyond their comprehension"; and poet Ted Hughes, who became poet laureate of England, showed "the pretensions of civilization" (Peck and Coyle, 275, 283). One writer who did not regard society as the cause of an individual's evil was William Golding, whose *Lord of the Flies* became an extremely popular book in the 1950s and 1960s. Huxley seems to have read few, if any, of these authors, since he was more involved with scientists and social thinkers. He admitted in a 1959 interview "that he had little interest in contemporary fiction" (Murray, 388), although he had read Jack Kerouac's *On the Road*, which he declared was boring, stating that "the road seemed to be awfully long," and works by British writer Kingsley Amis, whom he thought was "repeating himself" (Murray, 389, 388).

Besides writers, musicians were also taking a stand against the status quo. A new style of music called rock 'n' roll became popular with teenagers in the mid-1950s, with Elvis Presley as the leading artist. Probably the greatest impact on the arts in the 1960s was created by the new rock group that came from Liverpool, England—the Beatles—who became the most popular singers in rock music history. Although Huxley did not comment on rock 'n' roll, it seems very doubtful that he would have enjoyed this kind of music, because he felt that the classical music of Bach, Mozart, and Beethoven was the best type (Bedford 670, 673).

For Huxley, this dangerous but interesting and ever-changing world came to an end on November 22, 1963, a day that sent the nation into mourning when President John F. Kennedy was assassinated as he traveled by motorcade through Dallas, Texas. A few hours after the president's death, Aldous Huxley died of cancer in his Los Angeles home.

THE WORDS *BRAVE NEW WORLD* CONJURE UP A TECHNOLOGICALLY ADVANCED WORLD IN WHICH PEOPLE WILLINGLY GIVE UP THEIR FREEDOM.

Chapter 3

Brave New World

Brave New World is one of the most famous utopian novels ever written. It is actually a dystopian or anti-utopian book. As Huxley told a friend, "I am writing a novel about the future—on the horror of the Wellsian Utopia and a revolt against it" (*Letters*, 348). H. G. Wells, a friend of both Aldous and Julian Huxley, was a highly respected writer who popularized the idea that technological progress would result in a glorious future in books such as his 1923 novel, *Men Like Gods*. Huxley used his friend's socialistic, secular Utopia with its scientific methods of genetic engineering and birth control to create his *Brave New World*'s "wholly secular culture, dominated by economics, supported by technology, and dedicated to the—within carefully set limits—Freudian pleasure principle with its emphasis on libidinal appetite" (Baker, 97). He shows that the "search for Nirvana, like the search for Utopia or the end of history or the classless society, is ultimately a futile and dangerous one. It involves, if it does not necessitate, the sleep of reason. There is no escape from anxiety and struggle" (Hitchens, xxi).

Although *Brave New World* is set in the future, Huxley's novel is, as George Orwell observed, "a brilliant caricature of the present" (quoted in Hitchens, ix) in which he "only uses the lens of future time . . . in order to discover better the latent diseases of the here and now" (Firchow, 119). Huxley was convinced that one of the biggest problems in the modern world was that people were willingly giving up their freedom and their essential humanity to governmental control.

Since loss of freedom is also the issue that George Orwell explores in *Nineteen Eighty-Four*, the two novels have often been compared, but whereas Huxley's characters willingly give up their freedom, in Orwell's society, the masses are coerced into obedience and conformity through a police state run by a violent dictator called Big Brother. Although Huxley felt his former student's novel was "profoundly important," he thought his own view of world control was a more accurate prophecy of the future, stating, "My own belief is that the ruling oligarchy will find less arduous and wasteful ways of governing and of satisfying its lust for power, and that these ways will resemble those which I described in *Brave New World*" (*Letters*, 604). Huxley's vision that people would be controlled through conditioning and learn to love servitude "would indeed seem much more in line with what has actually happened in the West in the second half of the twentieth century" (Murray, 380); however, Orwell's view of a ruling class maintaining control through violence and imprisonment has been the prevailing method in non-Western countries in the twentieth century. Both works offer frightening predictions of mindless masses controlled by a powerful few—trends that continue today.

Although *Brave New World* is a highly serious study of society, Huxley described the book to his father as "a comic, or at least satirical, novel about the Future [*sic*], showing the appallingness (at any rate by our standards) of Utopia and adumbrating [outlining] the effects of thought and feeling of such quite possible biological inventions as the production of children in bottles (with consequent, abolition of the family and all the Freudian 'complexes' for which family relationships are responsible), the prolongation of youth, the devising of some harmless but effective substitute for alcohol, cocaine, opium etc.—and also the effects of such sociological reforms on Pavlovian conditioning of all children from birth and before birth, universal peace, security and stability" (*Letters*, 351).

Huxley's novel, then, is a terrifying look at a world in which science and technology are used by powerful rulers to control the masses, making them into mindless automatons. Set in the future but concerned with the present time, it is filled with comic and satiric elements that make readers laugh even as they witness the dissolution of the human spirit.

Plot

In the year 632 After Ford (A.F.), the Director of Hatcheries and Conditioning is giving students a tour of the London Hatcheries while explaining the benefits of the modern world. He shows them how the unborn, or "undecanted," babies growing in bottles are efficiently produced on a factory production line, where the embryos are socially predestined and conditioned by being given mixtures of chemicals to enable them to take their assigned places in the caste system. After decantation, the babies are subjected to intensive behaviorist conditioning to make everyone think alike, using Pavlov's methods and hypnopaedia (sleep teaching). With the arrival of Mustapha Mond, one of the ten World Controllers, the students learn the history of their culture as he tells them about old things, such as families and wars. He concludes by informing the students that the Controllers decided that conditioning instead of force was the way to control violent emotions.

The scene shifts to two of Mond's factory workers, Lenina Crowne and Henry Foster, who have been dating one another almost exclusively for four months. When Fanny, another factory worker, advises Lenina to follow society's rules and be promiscuous, Lenina decides to also date Bernard Marx, a deformed but intelligent man who is discontented with society. They plan to take a trip to the Savage Reservation in New Mexico. When Bernard visits the Director to get permission to travel, he learns that the Director took a trip to the reservation several decades earlier with a woman who had gotten lost and had never returned, and he discovers that the Director is thinking of deporting him to Iceland because of his nonconformist attitudes.

At the dirty, smelly reservation, Lenina and Bernard meet John, a blond, fair-skinned man whose mother, Linda, had come from London with a man named "Tomakin," John's father, who left her behind. John explains that he has always been isolated from the others because of his skin color and his mother's promiscuity. He also reveals that he knows how to read and owns two books—the works of William Shakespeare and the instructions for Beta Embryo-Storage Workers. He immediately falls in love with the alluring Lenina.

Much to their pleasure, Bernard takes John and Linda back to London with Lenina and him. When the Director prepares to banish Bernard, Bernard introduces Linda and John, who calls the Director "My father" (*Brave New World*, 140), causing the Director to resign in shame. While Linda is shunned because she is an old, obese, homely mother, John, who is also called "the Savage," becomes an immediate celebrity. As John's guardian, Bernard becomes popular, and he delights in his newfound importance. But John quickly becomes disillusioned with this society and soon refuses to go to Bernard's parties, which destroys Bernard's reputation. During this time, Lenina has become infatuated with John. When she makes sexual advances, he no longer idolizes her and angrily drives her away. After Linda dies from an overdose of the drug soma, John, highly agitated, destroys the soma being given to some lower caste members and tries to make them understand that it is a poison. A riot results, and Bernard and Helmholtz Watson, another discontented intellectual, try to help the Savage.

After the police restore order, the three rebels appear before Mustapha Mond. He and John exchange ideas about civilization, with the Controller defending the present system of society and John condemning it. Bernard and Helmholtz are exiled to an island, but the Controller, wanting to do more experimentation with the Savage, refuses to let John go with them.

Not wishing to be the subject of experiments, John retreats to a deserted lighthouse outside London, where the people from London pursue him. When Henry and Lenina arrive with others, John joins the hysterical crowd in "a long-drawn frenzy of sensuality" (230). The next day, he realizes what he has done and hangs himself.

Themes

In *Brave New World*, Huxley is more interested in presenting ideas than in developing plot and characters, making the book a "novel of ideas." It presents a prophetic warning of what might happen to the human spirit if scientific advances are used by a totalitarian government.

The Advancement of Science as It Affects Human Beings

In his 1946 foreword to *Brave New World*, Huxley stated that the "theme of *Brave New World* is not the advancement of science as such; it is the advancement of science as it affects human individuals." He elaborated on this idea by explaining that he was concerned only with "the sciences of life"—biology, physiology, and psychology—because they can result in a "really revolutionary revolution" that takes place "in the souls and flesh of human beings." *Brave New World* is based on his premise that "a really efficient totalitarian state would be one in which the all-powerful executive of political bosses and their army of managers control a population of slaves who do not have to be coerced, because they love their servitude"

("Preface," 8, 11). Huxley divides his theme into two parts: first, he details how governments can design and control their subjects, and, second, he analyzes whether these measures bring real happiness to the people.

Part 1: The Power of Dictators When Given the Resources of Advanced Science

Throughout the novel, Huxley portrays the way in which the citizens of the new world-state are manipulated by ten World Controllers who have learned to use science and technology to produce "a race which loves its servitude, a race of standardized machine-minders for standardized machines who will never challenge their authority. The . . . thinking and spiritual man has been sacrificed in his entirety" (Bowering, 8).

Huxley felt that one method governments would invent to make the masses love servitude is "a fully developed science of human differences, enabling government managers to assign any given individual to his or her proper place in the social and economic hierarchy" ("Preface," 12). The Fordian society accomplishes this in two ways: controlling people's genetic makeup before birth and conditioning them after birth.

To control genetic makeup, the leaders incorporate another method that Huxley felt was essential in making people love servitude: "a foolproof system of eugenics, designed to standardize the human product" (Huxley, "Preface," 12). In the *Brave New World* society, embryos are separated into five groups before they are born, forming a caste system of superiors—the Alphas and Betas—and inferiors—the Gammas, Deltas, and Epsilons. To create the top groups, biologically superior sperm are selected to fertilize biologically superior ova, which then receive excellent prenatal treatment. On the other hand, the lower castes, which include the majority of the unborn children, come from inferior eggs and sperm that are made into a

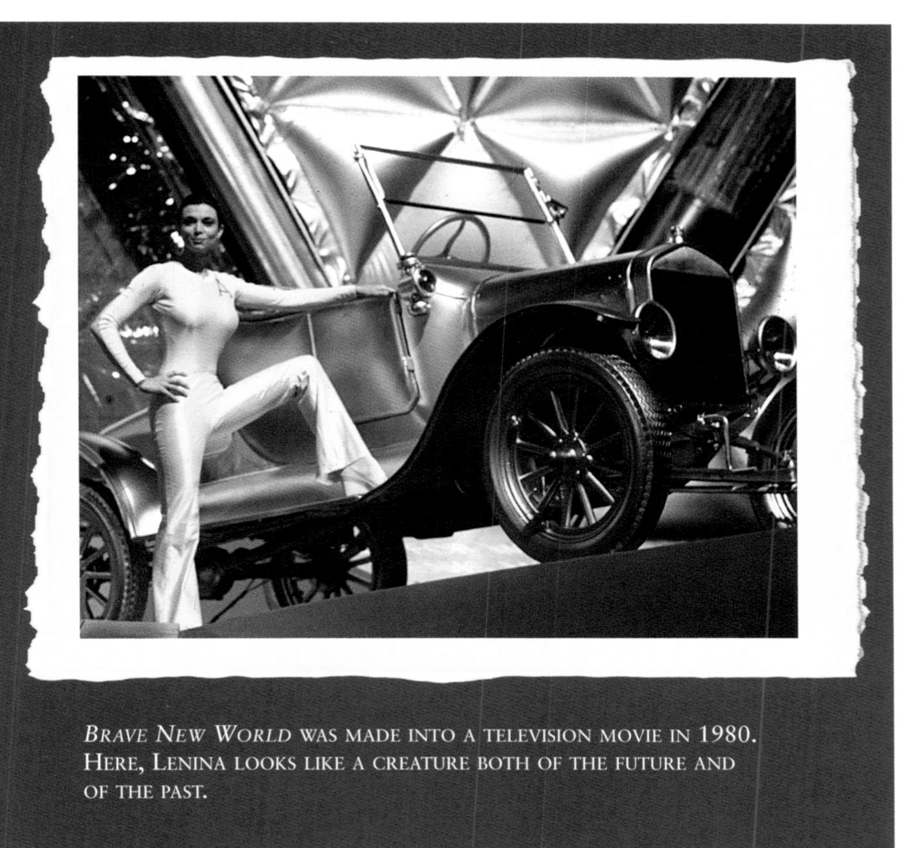

Brave New World was made into a television movie in 1980. Here, Lenina looks like a creature both of the future and of the past.

multiple number of twins by the Bokanovsky Process. Work can now be done by identical people doing identical jobs, making this process "one of the major instruments of social stability" (18). To further ensure their inferiority, they are injected prenatally with alcohol and other types of poisons. Therefore, the Fordian society, through genetic engineering, has been able to produce standardized humans—a small number of thinkers and a huge number of identical inferior creatures. Since the people of each caste have been eugenically developed to be satisfied to carry out their assigned tasks, the leaders have taken the first step to make sure that there are not "round pegs in square holes [which] tend to have dangerous thoughts about the social system and to infect others with their discontentments" (Huxley, "Preface," 12).

The World Controllers' second step toward making people love servitude occurs through what Huxley described as "a greatly improved technique of suggestion—through infant conditioning" ("Preface," 12). Following decantation, the rulers begin to brainwash infants and children, conditioning them with Pavlovian techniques, as seen with the eight-month-old Delta babies in the Neo-Pavlovian Conditioning Rooms. Children are also programmed through hypnopaedia to create "Community, Identity, and Stability," the motto of the Fordian state.

Sleep teaching promotes community as the children are conditioned with slogans that teach them that they are all necessary parts of one big community. "Every one belongs to every one else" (52, 114, 186) is one of the basic premises of *Brave New World*. Not only do the inhabitants belong to everyone sexually, but also they belong to one another as working members of the state, as their slogan "Every one works for every one else" (90) shows. Since they all are needed, "Everybody's happy now" (77, 78, 90), a motto that helps the citizens feel contented with their shallow lives. In addition, they learn that everything that happens is good since "Ford's in his flivver. All's well with the world" (49), words adapted from the Christian slogan, "God's in his heaven. All's well with the world."

Identity is formed by giving sleep lessons in class consciousness, such as the one taught to Beta children: "Alpha children wear grey. They work much harder than we do, because they're so frightfully clever. I'm really awfully glad I'm a Beta, because I don't work so hard. And then we are much better than the Gammas and Deltas. Gammas are stupid. They all wear green, and Delta children wear khaki. Oh no, I *don't* want to play with Delta children. And Epsilons are still worse. They're too stupid . . ." (35).

Stability is also ensured through sleep teaching. To have economic stability, the leaders brainwash citizens to spend money continually on new items instead of repairing old ones with sayings such as "Ending is better than mending" (54) and "The more stitches, the less riches" (55, 114). Physical well-being, also needed for stability, is guaranteed by giving elementary lessons in hygiene with slogans such as "Civilization is sterilization" (114) and "Cleanliness is next to fordliness" (105), a direct parallel to the Western saying, "Cleanliness is next to godliness." Fordians are encouraged to see doctors because "A doctor a day keeps the jim-jams away" (170).

Emotional stability is achieved with slogans used to abolish individualism because "When the individual feels, the community reels" (92). It is also brought about by using slogans to make people desire drugs and, therefore, eliminate emotions. "A gramme is better than a damn" (61, 89, 110, 177) encourages citizens to take drugs to get rid of hostile feelings, while "One cubic centimeter cures ten gloomy sentiments" (89) and "A gramme in time saves nine" (89) (an ironic revision of "A stitch in time saves nine") promote drug use to get rid of sadness. Emotional stability is also achieved by teaching slogans that make people feel contented because they are constantly pursuing pleasures. "Never put off till tomorrow the fun you can have today" (92) is a reversal of the present-day motto that encourages people to work hard every day, "Do not put off for tomorrow what you can do today," while the slogan "Nothing can be achieved without perseverance" (171) has been corrupted to mean that males and females must be promiscuous because they cannot know who will satisfy them unless they try out everyone.

Clearly the *Brave New World* society has learned to effectively teach morals and values to its members in order to promote "community, identity, and stability" through hypnopaedia, which the Director accurately calls "the greatest moralizing and socializing force of all time" (36).

A third way the Controllers make people love servitude is to provide, as Huxley says, "a substitute for alcohol and the other narcotics, something at once less harmful and more pleasure-giving than gin or heroin" ("Preface," 12). The Controllers use chemical persuasion by encouraging the people to use soma, "the most powerful instrument of authority in the hands of the Controllers of the World-state" (Bowering, 10). Not only do they promote drug use through the slogans learned through hypnopaedia, but they also make sure it is free and readily available. As Huxley related in *Brave New World Revisited*, "The systematic drugging of individuals for the benefit of the State (and incidentally, of course, for their own delight) was a main plank in the policy of the World Controllers. The daily Soma ration was an insurance against personal maladjustment, social unrest and the spread of subversive ideas. . . . [T]he drug had power to console and compensate, it called up visions of another, better world, it offered hope, strengthened faith and promoted charity" (297).

As a fourth way to keep the people under their power, the Controllers promote self-indulgence. Besides using sleep teaching to make the citizens desire nonstop activities during their leisure hours, the Controllers provide an assortment of games, movies called the feelies, the cabaret, and Solidarity Services. The people's biggest form of self-indulgence is through sexual freedom, which is made acceptable by the abolition of the family. The rulers use scientific advances to make sexual promiscuity possible by sterilizing most women, making them "freemartins" who cannot get pregnant. For the others, they have created contraceptives, and they hold Malthusian drills three times a week to make sure women remember to use them.

To persuade the people to be promiscuous, the rulers rely not only on hypnopaedia but also on music. For example, the Solidarity Service hymn, "Ford, we are twelve; oh, make us one, / Like drops within the Social River" (82–83), is a song asking for sexual oneness instead of spiritual unity. The popular tune, "Hug me till you drug me, honey; / Kiss me till I'm in a coma: / Hug me, honey, snuggly bunny; / Love's as good as *soma*" (153, 176, 181), promotes sex by suggesting that it can be as exhilarating as using drugs. In spite of the fact that the leaders promote sexual activity, they do not want the masses to experience love, a strong passion that causes instability; therefore, the only romantic song of the *Brave New World*, "Bottle of mine, it's you I've always wanted! / Bottle of mine, why was I ever decanted?" (79), tells of a person's love for the womb-type bottle that the unborn babies are grown in instead of love for a person.

The Fordian rulers, then, are experts at using the resources of advanced biology, psychology, and technology to enslave the masses. Through eugenics, conditioning (both Pavlovian and hypnopaedia), drugs, and the promotion of self-indulgence, the masses are led to believe that they are happy. In the Fordian world, "the imprisonment of the human spirit by science is almost complete; human values have totally disappeared, natural impulses allowed to atrophy until the inhabitants react like automata" (Bowering, 12).

Part 2: The Cost of Stability and Happiness

The results of letting dictators use scientific methods to control people are summarized in a debate on happiness between the Savage and Mustapha Mond in chapters sixteen and seventeen, a topic one critic regards as "perhaps, the most important thematic point in *Brave New World*" (Matter, 67). In order to have stability, which is the basis for happiness in Utopia, the Controller claims that art, scientific progress, religion, and ultimately freedom must all be sacrificed.

John, revolted by the poverty of art and culture in the *Brave New World* society, suggests to Mond that people should read and watch Shakespeare. All of his life he has been bombarded with the childish music and literature of the world-state through Linda. Having no knowledge of literature, she can only repeat jingles like "The cat is on the mat. The tot is in the pot" (121, 182), a verse taken from a children's reading lesson that regards a baby growing in a bottle as being as normal as a cat sitting on a mat. Another favorite, "A, B, C, Vitamin D. The fat's in the liver, the cod's in the sea" (125–126, 182, 184, 185), is a propaganda ditty to coerce people to take vitamins, with liver and cod being two good sources of vitamin D. Two of Linda's songs are revisions of nursery rhymes, and both reflect the tawdry culture of the Utopia. "Streptocock-Gee to Banbury-T, to see a fine bathroom and WC" (114, 182), was originally "Ride a cock horse to Banbury Cross / To see a fine lady upon a white horse / With rings on her fingers and bells on her toes / She shall have music wherever she goes." In the Fordian world, the magical world of Banbury Cross is reduced to a bathroom and a water closet (WC), another name for a toilet. "Bye Baby Banting, soon you'll need decanting" (116), like its model, "Bye, Baby Bunting, / Daddy's gone a' hunting. / He will get a rabbit skin / To wrap the baby bunting in," is about a newborn baby, but the Fordian baby comes from an indifferent bottle, while the original baby has a loving father who is seeking to provide a soft blanket for his newborn.

John has found the *Brave New World* adult reading material to be hardly any better. There are manuals to guide workers, such as Linda's *The Chemical and Bacteriological Conditioning for the Embryo, Practical Instructions for Beta Embryo Store Workers*, and Henry

LOVE IS THE ENEMY OF CONTROL. THOSE WHO RUN THE GOVERNMENT IN *BRAVE NEW WORLD* KNOW THAT. JOHN AND LENINA'S LOVE SIMPLY CANNOT SURVIVE.

Ford's *My Life and Work, by Our Ford.* John has also experienced the art of the Fordian culture—the gross feelies. It is no wonder that he hates what passes for art and literature in this society and advocates that Shakespeare be made available to the masses. Even though Mond agrees with the Savage that "*Othello*'s better than those feelies," he insists that "you've got to choose between happiness and what people used to call high art" because "that's the price we have to pay for stability" (199).

Social stability and happiness are also the reasons Mond gives for keeping science "most carefully chained and muzzled" (203). The discussion of science begins when John, appalled at the "horrible" Delta "twin-herds" that act like "human maggots," asks the Controller why he does not use science to make everyone into "an Alpha Double Plus" (200). Mond explains that a "society of Alphas couldn't fail to be unstable and miserable. . . . An Alpha-decanted, Alpha-conditioned man would go mad if he had to do Epsilon Semi-Moron work—go mad, or start smashing things up" (200). Not only does Mond refrain from using known scientific methods to create ideal individuals, but he also refuses to use scientific advances to make work easier or work hours shorter: "We don't want to change. Every change is a menace to stability. That's another reason why we're so chary of applying new inventions. Every discovery in pure science is potentially subversive; even science must sometimes be treated as a possible enemy. Yes, even science" (202).

Religion, Mustapha Mond continues, is the third enemy of stability and happiness. Although Mond admits that John may be right that there is a God, he is convinced that people cannot hear about him because "God isn't compatible with machinery and scientific medicine and universal happiness" (210). When John points out, "if you allowed yourselves to think of God, you wouldn't allow yourselves to be degraded by pleasant vices. You'd have a reason for bearing things patiently, for doing things with courage. . . . You'd have a reason for self-denial. . . . You'd have a reason for chastity" (212), Mond explains that these have all been eliminated from civilization because they lead to passion, instability, and war.

With the loss of art, scientific progress, and religion comes the loss of freedom, something the Savage refuses to give up. At the end of the debate, Mond is still committed to making the citizens live in a state of childish happiness, while John adamantly insists that this type of happiness is too great a price to pay: "I want God, I want poetry, I want real danger, I want freedom, I want goodness. I want sin" (215). Although Mond points out that this means he is "claiming the right to be unhappy," John responds, "I claim them all" (215). By the end of the debate, when John discovers that Mond's society "must censor art, restrain individuality, do away with love, and prohibit innovation in order to maintain stability," he understands "that the myth and the reality of utopia are very different indeed" (Matter, 69).

As Huxley makes clear, this new world order is not Utopia because "such a world must give up not only war, but also spiritual conflicts of any kind, not only superstition, but also religion, not only literary criticism, but also great creative art of whatever kind, not only economic chaos, but also all the beauty of the old traditional things, not only the hard and ugly parts of ethics, but the tender and beautiful parts too" (Needham, 59).

The Human Desire to Conform

Although the advancement of science as it affects human beings is Huxley's primary theme, he includes several minor themes as well. One is people's yearning to conform in order to be accepted by others. Hardly any one raised in the Fordian society finds fault with doing and thinking the same as everyone else. Although it looks as if Lenina might be a nonconformist when she expresses a desire to date only one man, she quickly agrees to act as expected and begins dating Bernard as well as Henry. Bernard and Mustapha Mond, two Alpha-Pluses, the most intelligent members of this society, would rather conform than leave society. Even outsider John, although a rebel against the world-state, desires to conform to the brutal reservation society. Only Helmholtz embraces total individuality, and he is ostracized. What Huxley shows is that when everyone thinks and acts alike, there is no room for the individual.

People's Admiration for Science and Indifference Toward the Humanities

Another minor theme is Huxley's concern about people's undue respect for science and technology and their dismissal of the arts and humanities. In the Brave New World society, science, and technology become the religion. The Fordians have gained many benefits from technology—more pleasures, greater comforts, healthier lives—but, as a result, they have lost imagination. They are no longer resourceful or creative because they have given up the arts, humanities, and religion. Therefore, the whole person no longer exists.

Women as Second-Class Citizens

Even though women are freed from some onerous tasks such as housework, women's inferior position to men is apparent in this novel, which was written decades before the women's liberation movement began. Critic June Deery notes that "on occasion, [Huxley] does recognize and explicitly criticize women's treatment in this society" (132), such as when the Director patronizingly pats Lenina on her behind and murmurs, "Charming,

charming," while she responds with a "rather deferential smile" (26), and when the men discuss Lenina as a piece of "meat" (51) or nonchalantly advise acquaintances "to try her" (51) sexually.

But Deery points out that Huxley usually does not denounce the sexual injustices. His men are the leaders of society. Even the science students in the first chapters are male, while the women are helpmates, serving as nurses, teachers, secretaries, and factory workers. The men are in charge of dating—they ask the women out, and they drive the helicopters. The Alpha male lovers—the Director, Henry, and Bernard—belong to a higher caste than Linda and Lenina, both Betas. The men are smarter than the women, who always ask the questions, such as Lenina's inquiry, "Why do the smoke-stacks have those things like balconies around them?" And the men always know the answers, "'Phosphous recovery,' explained Henry telegraphically" (76). No woman in Huxley's Utopia has power. In fact, the women are so powerless that they do not seem to be able to say "no" to sex. Therefore, when Lenina wants to be with John, she takes soma to tolerate having sex with a high-caste man who desires her. The feelies also show the woman's inferior position, for the blond Beta becomes the appreciative lover of her three rescuers. Even women's natural role as the reproductive members of society has been taken away—male scientists now grow babies in bottles while the women are either sterilized or trained to use contraceptives. Meanwhile, the men's sexuality is not altered (Deery, 131–136). The women seem to be totally passive members of society who are desired only as sexual beings.

Analysis

Setting

Huxley sets his book in A.D. 2540, or, as he calls it, 632 After Ford, the era that began with the introduction of Our Ford's first Model T in 1908. There are two locations: the Fordian society of London and the Savage Reservation in New Mexico.

Huxley describes the London society in ironic terms. The first chapter, in which new life is created, is set in a cold, impersonal factory that has "dead and frozen light, corpse-coloured workers each performing his part to bring into the world new life which, if all goes well, will be spiritually dead, or at least debased" (May, 105). The irony continues as "the party moves to the sunny nurseries in which takes place a systematic removal of any budding love of nature to ensure that shades of the prison-house close earlier and more irreversibly than they otherwise would" (May, 105). London is seen as a sterile city physically, emotionally, and spiritually.

The primitive society on the Indian Reservation is also far from glamorous. Huxley ironically names it "Malpais," using the French words *mal pays*, which mean "evil country" or "bad place" (Sisk, 125). With "its ceremonies, superstitions, diseases, the repellent features of its aged folk, the smells, lice, dead dogs, snakes, the lastingness of the brightly-coloured but often filthy clothes, the murderous sexual possessiveness" (May, 110), it does not offer an attractive alternative to the Fordian culture.

Looking closely, the tribal society and the utopian one "actually mirror each other in a number of ways. History is no more relevant to the inhabitants of the reservation than to the citizens of Fordian civilization. Both societies are morally coercive, while the debasing violence of the fertility ritual finds its attenuated counterpart in the repressed violence of the communal orgies of Bernard's London" (Baker, 99). Huxley calls both societies "queer and abnormal," the utopian world offering a life of "insanity" and the Indian village offering one of "lunacy" ("Preface," 6).

Structure

Brave New World consists of two parts of nine chapters each. The first half introduces the two societies in London, chapters one through six, and New Mexico, chapters seven through nine. Huxley does not start with a plot but with exposition, devoting his first two chapters to explanations of the main elements of social control used in London's Fordian society. In the third chapter, Huxley continues the exposition but also begins the plot by introducing three main characters—Mustapha Mond, Bernard Marx, and Lenina Crowne. The chapter is organized by paragraphs that alternate between Mond's statements and the conversations taking place among the Hatchery workers as they are getting ready for leisure activities. This technique enables Huxley to contrast "the stable behaviorist present of the World State with its unstable neurotic past" (Baker, 117).

After this long exposition, Huxley develops his plot by focusing on Bernard and Lenina. Both chapters four and five are divided into two parts that focus first on Lenina and then on Bernard, in order to "compare the two characters, the perfectly-adjusted girl who wholeheartedly enjoys her helicopter trip followed by a visit to a cabaret, and the miserably peculiar man who first pours out his grievances to a friend, Helmholtz Watson, and then feels alone at a Solidarity Service" (May, 107). Chapter six is the transition from the Fordian to the primitive society as Bernard takes Lenina to the Indian Reservation. In the next three chapters, seven through nine, Huxley shifts his focus to life on the reservation, particularly looking at the Savage and his mother.

The second half of the book, chapters ten through eighteen, tells the story of the stranger, John, being introduced to a new society. In chapter ten, Huxley moves his plot along as John and Linda are introduced to the Director. Chapters eleven and twelve are subdivided into sections describing Bernard's snobbish enjoyment of his popularity, Linda's use of soma, Lenina's desire for John and his love for her, and his growing disgust with the world-state. The situations come to a head in the displays of violence in the next three chapters, thirteen through fifteen, as John attacks Lenina when she wants sex, strikes the children watching his mother die, and causes a riot by destroying the soma that is being given out to Delta workers.

Although these scenes are quite comical, the interviews with Mustapha Mond in chapters sixteen and seventeen are totally serious and thoughtful, as John and the Controller debate their views on civilization, enabling Huxley to tell "the reader as openly as possible what the alternatives are" (May, 114). The novel ends with John leaving London, being harassed by sightseers, engaging in sexual activities, and committing suicide.

The Characters

Even though Huxley had trouble making his characters into fully developed entities, admitting, "I'm not very good at creating people; I don't have a very wide repertory of characters" (quoted in Watt, 134), prominent Huxley scholar Peter Edgerly Firchow is convinced that Huxley's characters "are not merely made of cardboard and papier-mâché. That they are nonetheless not full and complete human beings is quite true; but for all the technology and conditioning and impulses toward uniformity, there is still something profoundly human about them" (Firchow, in Bloom, 114).

Lenina begins as a typical Beta woman interested in her looks, sex, and thoughtless amusements. A number of times she describes herself as "pneumatic," a term Huxley borrows from T. S. Eliot's "Whispers of Immortality" in which plump female bodies give "promise of pneumatic bliss" (quoted in Hitchens, xiii). In *Brave New World*, it is a coarse word used "by both its male and female characters as a cheap synonym for good sex" (Hitchens, xiii). For Lenina, the word means that she has a well-rounded body, particularly her bosom, which the men find desirable. Although Lenina "seems at first to be nothing more than a pretty and addle-brained young woman without any emotional depth whatever," Firchow demonstrates that she changes when she falls in love and becomes one of Huxley's fairly complex characters (Firchow, in Bloom, 112–113). After seeing the feelies, she wants to seduce John and is puzzled when he innocently sends her home in a taxicopter. As her love for John grows, she becomes more and more impatient with Henry, and she refuses to follow Fanny's advice to see other men. The final sad but comic scenes between Lenina and the Savage show her inability to understand any values other than her own. When she realizes that John loves her, she does what she thinks is normal and unzips her clothes in preparation for sex; she cannot understand John's angry response. In their last encounter at the lighthouse, Lenina, unintentionally pressing her hand over her heart indicating her love, once again wants sex, and, just as before, flees in terror when he attacks her. Lenina, then, is a victim of her emotionless society, so strongly conditioned that she cannot understand true passion.

The antihero Bernard Marx "oscillates between a despairing conformity and a servile endorsement of Fordean [sic] values" (Baker, 100). At the beginning of the novel, this Alpha-Plus man seems to be the perfect rebel against the World Society, even though he is physically deformed, being too small and too dark for his caste because "somebody made a mistake when he was still in the bottle—thought he was a Gamma and put alcohol into his blood-surrogate" (51). He "rejects the sterile assumptions of his culture. He 'doesn't like Obstacle Golf'; he even likes to be alone; and he joins in the soma battle with his anarchist friends" (Holmes, 30). Furthermore, he is able to imagine and even look for true love instead of sexual pleasure. Although this unhappy misfit rails against society, he, at the same time, wants to be admired by his fellow citizens. Therefore, he is a braggart who tries to assert his superiority, and, when he gets the chance to be popular, he happily embraces the Fordian society. By the end, he has become "weak and cowardly and vain" because he "is willing to settle for less because it is so much easier than trying to strive for more" (Firchow, in Bloom, 112).

Handsome Helmholtz Watson has been a very successful player in the Fordian society. Besides being good at his job, this Alpha-Plus male is a desirable lover and an expert sportsman. But he is unhappy, looking for something to make his life fulfilling. Unlike Bernard, Helmholtz actually wants to leave the conformist society and chooses to be exiled to the frigid Falkland Islands, where he "will not only have solitude but also a harsh climate in which to suffer and to gain new and very different experiences" so that he can write better poetry (Firchow, in Bloom, 111). He is the only one who "hopes for creative self-fulfillment" (Holmes, 30).

The real hero of the book is John the Savage, who belongs neither to the New Mexican nor the London society. He is rejected by the primitive community since he is the son of Fordian parents, but he is also unfit for the *Brave New World* since he has knowledge of love, passions, and family ties that he learned on the Indian Reservation and through his reading of Shakespeare. Naïve and simple, he has no idea when he leaves the reservation that he will be entering a society in which emotions, culture, religion, individuality, and freedom are all sacrificed for the sake of peace and one-dimensional happiness.

Linda is an outcast in both the primitive and the Fordian societies. Her conditioning has made her totally unfit to adjust to motherhood, monogamy, old age, or the deprivations that she finds on the Indian Reservation. In London, she is shunned not only because she is a mother but also because she has grown old, fat, and ugly. Therefore, she is allowed to overdose on soma and die in her dream world.

Although he is diplomatic and polite, Mustapha Mond, one of the ten World Controllers, is a menacing figure whose rule is absolute. He reveals that he, as a young man, had to choose between his own happiness, which meant nonconformity and exile, and the happiness of others, which meant conformity and society. He chose to stay in civilization but still muses on what he has given up. When looking at a paper entitled "A New Theory of Biology," he reflects, "What fun it would be . . . if one didn't have to think about happiness!" (162). He is "the chilly, objective theorist of the idea that social engineering and the wide distribution of easy pleasure will keep the masses in line" (Hitchens, x).

The Use of Humor

Science-fiction historian Brian Aldiss asks, "Isn't one of the delights of [Huxley's *Brave New World*], when all is said and pontificated, that it is told with a perfect balance of wit and humour?" (Aldiss and Wingrove, 185). Huxley's sense of humor is not only apparent in the plot, with funny elements such as Lenina's inability to understand that she is falling in love or the riot scene at the hospital, but also in Huxley's "puns and plays on words [which] always gave him special pleasure" (Gervas Huxley, 58).

Sometimes Huxley creates broad humor by making up words or using old words in new ways. Movies that people can feel as well as see and hear become "feelies." Instruments that play seductive jazz music are "sexophones," while an organ that emits odors is "The Finest Scent and Colour Organ" and the one that plays soothing music in the hospital is the "Super-Vox-Wurlitzeriana," named after the Wurlitzer organ used in churches. Thousands of siblings can be made in a short period time by ripening eggs in the ovary at once through "Podsnap's Technique," named after the self-important character Podsnap in Charles Dickens's *Our Mutual Friend*. Babies are no longer born but "decanted' like wine. Fordians enjoy "orgy-porgy," a parody of the nursery rhyme "Georgie Porgie," which now refers to group sex. London's exclusive club for male intellectuals, the Athenaeum Club, has turned into the "Aphroditeum Club," named for the Greek goddess of beauty, fertility, and sexual love.

Another way Huxley creates humor is by making up pompous titles. One factory worker is called the "Human Element Manager and Assistant Fertilizer-General"; the writing department is the "College of Emotional Engineering"; and cow pastures are part of the "Internal and External Secretion Trust." Simple games are made to seem important with pretentious names: the children's ball game becomes "Centrifugal Bumble-puppy"; golf is "Obstacle and Electro-magnetic Golf Courts"; and play-off games are the "Semi-Demi-Finals of the Women's Heavyweight Wrestling Championship."

Besides making up ridiculous names, Huxley also uses puns. For instance, Henry Foster fosters new life as he "conducts ovarian research in the Hatchery, with the aim of producing increasing numbers of new workers" (Sisk, 124), and Fanny and Lenina Crowne are the two most desirable females; they are at the top or the crown.

One of the most frequent ways Huxley adds humor is by satirizing contemporary and historical people by incorporating their names into the names he gives his characters and objects. Huxley has little esteem for any prominent national leader. The types of governments that get the worst trouncing are socialism and Marxism, which Huxley regarded as "the latest variants of scientific rationalism, [which] differed from other varieties only in their greater arrogance and fanaticism" (Kumar, 243).

Huxley blasts the revolutionary left by changing two deadly Russian enemies, Vladimir Lenin, who led the Communist Russian Revolution, and Fanny Kaplan, who attempted to assassinate him, into friends, Lenina and Fanny. Although they have different opinions, in Ford's happy society in which everyone gets along, Lenina concludes their disagreement by saying, "Let's make peace, Fanny darling" (54). The co-authors of *The Communist Manifest*, Karl Marx and Friedrich Engels, are reduced to the two Brave New World conformists, the almost revolutionary Bernard Marx and the complacent Solidarity Service participant, Sarojini Engels. And Leon Trotsky, who believed in continuous revolution to establish worldwide socialism, becomes a little girl who wants continuous erotic pleasures, Polly Trotsky.

Huxley also had no time for right-wing dictators. He shows the danger of Controller Mustapha Mond by giving him the name of the forceful Turkish leader who compelled his country to become modern and secular, Mustapha Kemal Atatürk.

He even cuts down Herbert Hoover, the American president during the stock-market crash that led to the Great Depression, by giving his name to the non-thinkers Herbert Bakunin and Benito Hoover. Hoover not only has the president's surname, but he also has his "chubby red face" and his naivety, being "notoriously good-natured" (65). Combining the name of this complacent president with brutal revolutionaries, Mikhail Bakunin, the Russian founder of anarchism, and Benito Mussolini, the Fascist leader of Italy, makes these names even sillier.

Capitalists and leaders of technology also fall victim to Huxley's humor. His main target is Henry Ford, the founder of the American Ford Auto Company, who revolutionized factory production through the modern assembly line. He is cleverly converted into the Lord of the

Brave New World. Huxley also wittily gives Ford's first name to conventional Henry Foster, who has many of Ford's interests: he has "expert knowledge" of assembly lines (20), loves to fly fast-moving machines, and is extremely concerned that things be done rapidly and on time, much like Ford's concern for a fast-moving assembly line. He tells Lenina that she is "four minutes late" for their date and that the transatlantic Red Rocket was "seven minutes behind time" (66). Huxley's secondary capitalist target is Alfred Mond, a British businessman who founded one of the largest chemical companies in the world. Critic Krishan Kumar explains that "Mond stands for the new giant conglomerates that were coming to dominate the industrial world. He is a particularly good choice on Huxley's part, not simply as one of the new breed of scientist-industrialist, but because both the left and the right were hailing the conglomerates enthusiastically as the latest and most progressive organizational form in the modern world: the right because they were a move towards 'rationalization,' the left because they were a halfway- house to nationalization" (243). Huxley gives his last name to all-powerful Controller, Mustapha Mond.

As might be expected, scientists and economists fall prey to Huxley's acerbic pen. He blasts psychoanalyst Sigmund Freud, who promoted the idea that sexual activity outside marriage was necessary for human happiness, using his name interchangeably with "Ford," and, therefore, making him another Lord of the Brave New World. Huxley goes after Ivan Pavlov, the Russian pioneer of behavioral conditioning, with the Neo-Pavlovian Conditioning Rooms. He has fun with Thomas Malthus, an economist who warned about population growth, by providing the women with Malthusian belts to carry contraceptives. He teases Charles Darwin, the famous naturalist who popularized the theory of evolution, by combining his name with that of the mighty French leader

Napoleon Bonaparte and reducing him to Darwin Bonaparte, the big game photographer who subjects himself to various natural hardships in order to get good pictures. Huxley assigns the names of two prominent scientists to Helmholtz Watson; his first name comes from a nineteenth-century German physicist, Hermann von Helmholtz, while his surname is derived from an American behaviorist psychologist who experimented with conditioning in human beings, John B. Watson. (As an added dimension, his last name is also associated with Sir William Watson, an English poet.)

Huxley has fun with social theorists, too. In particular, he ridicules the Enlightenment philosopher Jean-Jacques Rousseau, who believed that an individual uncorrupted by society was an ideal person whom he called a "Noble Savage." Huxley not only names one of Lenina's boyfriends Jean-Jacques Habibullah, but he also calls John "the Savage," a man who is definitely noble but not a "savage," since he grew up learning Shakespeare. Ironically, the real savages are far from noble, living shabby lives filled with filth, disease, death, and religious and sexual perversions.

Writers are also mocked by Huxley. He pokes fun at utopian writer H. G. Wells with Dr. Wells, Fanny's doctor, who advises her to get a Pregnancy Substitute (44). But Huxley "reserves his harshest treatment for another famous Fabian Socialist, George Bernard Shaw" (Sisk, 126), giving his name to three people: conformist George Edzel, Linda's immoral Dr. Shaw, and smart but cowardly Bernard Marx, who refuses to stand up for his beliefs. Moreover, Huxley twice ridicules Shaw's writings, as critic David W. Sisk points out. First, "the Director of Hatcheries explains that the first discovery of hypnopaedia occurred when a radio left on overnight broadcast Shaw declaiming on the subject of his own genius, an address that a young Polish boy wakes up repeating, despite not understanding English. The ironic dig is clear. Shaw's words are merely inconsequential babble" (126). Second, "Shaw is 'one of the very few whose works have been permitted to come down to us,' as the Director notes. As Mond makes clear to the touring students, nearly all literature published before the year A.F. 150 has been suppressed; the fact that Shaw's works are not forbidden points to their essential harmlessness and their inability to disrupt conditioning"(126).

Huxley's use of historical and cultural figures provides a biting satire of his world and its leaders.

Motifs

"Our Ford" and Shakespeare are Huxley's two major motifs—recurring phrases, ideas, and literary devices that help develop themes.

Our Ford

"Our Lord" is turned into "Our Ford" in Huxley's world state in which religion has been replaced with a worship of technology. The new god is Henry Ford, who made the first efficient assembly line and cheap cars. In the essay "The Puritan" in *Music at Night*, Huxley explained how he used this motif: "'Fordism' . . . demands that we should sacrifice the animal man (and along with the animal large portions of the thinking, spiritual man) not indeed to God, but to the Machine. There is no place in the factory, or in that larger factory which is the modern industrialized world, for animals on the one hand, or for artists, mystics, or even, finally, individuals on the other. Of all the ascetic religions Fordism is that which demands the cruellest mutilations of the human psyche—demands the cruellest mutilations and offers the smallest spiritual returns" (quoted in Bowering, 8).

Huxley cleverly uses the name "Ford" for "Lord" throughout the novel. The novel takes place in the "Year of Our Ford" 632 After Ford, parodying The "Year of

In 1998, a new film version of *Brave New World* was produced. Here, the youngsters get an early look at conformity.

Our Lord," or "Anno Domini" (A.D.). The citizens substitute Ford's name for "Lord" in expressions such as "Oh, Ford," "For Ford's sake," "My Ford," "Ford help him," and "Ford helps those who help themselves." The Christian benediction becomes "Ford keep you!" (195). The citizens attend the "Ford's Day Solidarity Groups" instead of Christian religious services, and they go to the "Fordson Community Singery." The popular *Christian Science Monitor* has become the *Fordian Science Monitor*. And the Christian crosses have been turned into "Ts" to signify Ford's Model T car. Therefore, Lenina wears a golden T necklace, and the names of several places in England have changed—"Charing Cross" is now "Charing-T" and "Banbury Cross" is known as "Banbury-T." Even the famous English clock, "Big Ben," is changed to "Big Henry."

Shakespeare

The second major motif that Huxley uses is Shakespeare, "the symbol of the human spirit, opposed to Fordism and applied science" (Bowering, 12). He primarily refers to seven plays: *The Tempest*, *Troilus and Cressida*, and five of the bard's greatest tragedies—*Hamlet*, *Romeo and Juliet*, *Othello*, *Macbeth*, and *King Lear*.

With *The Tempest*, Huxley compares the wonderful possibilities that are open to civilization and the dark realities of that civilization. The novel gets its title from this play, and Huxley, like Shakespeare, uses the words *brave new world* ironically. When Shakespeare's innocent Miranda sees sinful men from a different civilization, she exclaims, "O wonder! / How many goodly creatures are there here! / How beauteous mankind is! O brave new world, / That has such people in't!" (5.1.183–186). John, like Miranda, is enthralled when he first sees civilized people (129–130), but, after he has lived in London, the "words mocked him derisively" (190).

Huxley continues the irony by using *The Tempest* to contrast true love with the passionless sex of the Fordian society. Believing Lenina to be virtuous, naïve John borrows the words of Miranda's lover, Ferdinand, to tell her how much he loves her: "Admired Lenina, indeed the top of admiration, worth what's dearest in the world. . . . So perfect and so peerless are created . . . of every creature's best" (172–173; *The Tempest* 3.1.37–39, 47–48). Like Ferdinand, John wants to do some great deed to prove himself worthy of her love: "There be some sports are painful—you know. . . . But some kinds of baseness are nobly undergone" (173; *The Tempest* 3.1.1–3). He promises that he will not sleep with her before marriage and "break her virgin knot before all sanctimonious ceremonies may with full and holy rite. . ." be performed (174; *The Tempest* 4.1.15–17), vowing that even "the murkiest den, the most opportune place . . . shall never melt mine honor into lust" (175; *The Tempest* 4.1.25–28). As Lenina becomes more alluring, John holds back his desires by remembering that "the strongest oaths are straw to the fire i' the blood. Be more abstemious, or else" (176; *The Tempest* 4.1.52–53). All of these virtuous sentiments are shattered when Lenina unzips her clothes and prepares for sex.

The Tempest is also used by John to compare aspects of Shakespeare's imaginative society to the London society. Although John likes the Fordian music and is delighted when Mond quotes from *The Tempest*—"Sometimes a thousand twangling instruments will hum about my ears and sometimes voices" (197; *The Tempest* 3.2.139–140)—he is unimpressed with the accomplishments of London civilization, such as the speed of a rocket: "Ariel [a spirit in *The Tempest*] could put a girdle round the earth in forty minutes" (146), he notes. Through this play, then, Huxley ironically contrasts an ideal society with the Brave New World one.

Huxley uses *Hamlet* to reveal John's hatred of corruption. John sees Linda and Popé's illicit relationship as similar to the unlawful marriage of Hamlet's uncle Claudius and his mother, railing that his mother has chosen "to live / In the rank sweat of an enseamed bed, / Stew'd in corruption, honeying and making love / Over the nasty sty" (123; *Hamlet* 3.4.93–96). John views his mother's lover as a villain like Claudius: "A man can smile and smile and be a villain. Remorseless, treacherous, lecherous, kindless villain" (123; *Hamlet* 1.5.109; 2.2.581). He would like to kill Popé, reflecting, like Hamlet, about when he will do it: "When he is drunk asleep, or in his rage / Or in the incestuous pleasure of his bed" (124; *Hamlet* 3.3.89–90).

Even though John hates corruption, he realizes that in order to truly live, people must be exposed to unpleasant things so that they, like Hamlet, are forced to decide "whether 'tis better in the mind to suffer the slings and arrows of outrageous fortune, or to take arms against a sea of troubles and by opposing end them" (214; *Hamlet* 3.1.58–61). John feels that life that is too easy is not worth living because true meaning is found by "exposing what is mortal and unsure to all that fortune, death and danger dare, even for an eggshell" (214; *Hamlet* 4.4.52–54). While taking a stand against corruption gives value to life, surrendering to corruption, as Linda does, causes a person to be less than human, becoming, as Hamlet says, nothing more than a "good kissing carrion" (226; *Hamlet* 2.2.182). Even though John, like sinful Claudius, prays for forgiveness for his own corruption (218; *Hamlet* 3.3.36–72), he worries that corruption may continue in dreams after death: "Sleep. Perchance to dream. . . . For in that sleep of death, what dreams?" (227; *Hamlet* 3.1.66–67). Huxley's use of Shakespeare's play about "something rotten in the state of Denmark" (*Hamlet* 1.4.90) shows that people need to struggle to overcome corruption.

Romeo and Juliet is used to compare the romantic love between Romeo and Juliet with the Savage's passionate feelings for Lenina, whom he sees as a new Juliet. Viewing her lovely body, John, not quite accurately, quotes Romeo: "On the white wonder of dear Juliet's hand, may seize / And steal immortal blessing from her lips, / Who, even in pure and vestal modesty, / Still blush, as thinking their own kisses sin" (134; *Romeo and Juliet* 3.3.36–39). He repeats Romeo's romantic sentiments about his love's perfection: "Oh, she doth teach the torches to burn bright! / It seems she hangs upon the cheek of night / Like a rich jewel in an Ethiope's ear; / Beauty too rich for use, for earth too dear" (163; *Romeo and Juliet* 1.5.45–48). As he rereads the play, "seeing himself as Romeo and Lenina as Juliet" (167), John emotionally reads Juliet's passionate plea when her parents try to force her to marry Paris and be separated from Romeo forever: "Is there no pity sitting in the clouds, / That sees into the bottom of my grief?" (168; *Romeo and Juliet* 3.5.198–203).

Once Lenina offers to have sexual relations with John, the magical spell of *Romeo and Juliet* is broken, and John quotes from *Othello*, revealing his violent passions of both love and hate for Lenina, the same emotions Othello felt for Desdemona. Thinking that Desdemona is false to him, Othello reviles her as a "whore" and "impudent strumpet," which are John's responses to Lenina (177, 178, 224, 225, 229; *Othello* 4.2.74, 83). John, like Othello, now looks at his loved one as "thou weed, who are so lovely fair and smell'st so sweet that the sense aches at thee. Was this most goodly book [fair paper] made to write 'whore' upon? Heaven stop the nose at it" (178; *Othello* 4.2.69–71, 73–74). John condemns the feelies, a gross retelling of the *Othello* story, by using Othello's words, "Goats and Monkeys," and implores the Controller to "let them see *Othello* instead" (198; *Othello* 4.1.268). He wants people to experience pain and hardship because these intensify pleasure, as Othello declares, "If after every tempest came such calms, may the winds blow till they have wakened death" (213; *Othello* 2.1.184–185). John uses *Othello* to show that strong emotions are necessary parts of an authentic life.

Huxley includes *Troilus and Cressida*, the tragic comedy about an idealistic man who loves a wanton woman, in much the same says as he uses both *Romeo and Juliet* and *Othello*. Like Romeo, Troilus is a romantic lover whom John quotes when he describes Lenina as bodily perfection: "Her eyes, her hair, her cheek, her gait, her voice, / Handlest in thy discourse, O, that her hand, / In whose comparison all whites are ink, / Writing their own reproach, to whose soft seizure / The cygnet's down is harsh" (134; *Troilus and Cressida* 1.1.56–60). Innocently, he assumes, like Troilus, that they will be forever devoted to each other, "outliving beauty's outward, with a mind that doth renew swifter than blood decays!" (174; *Troilus and Cressida* 3.2.161–162). When Lenina proves to be promiscuous like Cressida, John rails about "the devil Luxury with his fat rump and potato finger" (178; *Troilus and Cressida* 5.2.56–57) and yells, "Fry, lechery, fry!" (229; *Troilus and Cressida* 5.2.57–58). Now, knowing Lenina's true nature, he understands that all Londoners have sacrificed things of value for self-indulgent pleasures because he knows that "value dwells not in particular will. . . . It holds his estimate and dignity as well wherein 'tis precious of itself as in the prizer" (212; *Troilus and Cressida* 2.2.53–56).

Macbeth examines the intense emotions that come with pain, depression, and thoughts of death. John first uses it to depict physical pain, calling the bloodstains from the whipping during the primitive religious service as that "damned spot" (110; *Macbeth* 5.1.34) and explaining that if he had been the boy whipped he would have sacrificed so much blood that it could not be cleaned by "the multitudinous seas incarnadine" (111; *Macbeth*

2.2.66), Macbeth's words describing his bloody hands. He also uses *Macbeth* to express his emotional pain. Thinking of his despair after being stoned and ostracized by the Indian boys, John quotes Macbeth's speech, which was uttered in his depression after he learned of Lady Macbeth's death: "To-morrow and to-morrow and to-morrow" (127; *Macbeth* 5.5.19). When he is depressed and thinking about death, he recalls Macbeth's statement, "And all our yesterdays have lighted fools the way to dusty death" (226; *Macbeth* 5.5.22–23). In spite of these agonizing experiences with physical and emotional pain, John understands that even hurtful passions are essential to life and, therefore, condemns the emotionless feelies as tales "told by an idiot" (199; *Macbeth* 5.5.27), Macbeth's expression used to describe a meaningless life.

King Lear is quoted by John first to express rage against wicked people and, later, to show acceptance of all aspects of life. Revolted by Lenina, John rails against the sexual appetites of women, using Lear's words as he condemns his daughters, "The wren goes to't and the small gilded fly does lecher in my sight. . . . The fitchew nor the soiled horse goes to't with a more riotous appetite. Down from the waist they are Centaurs, though women all above. But to the girdle do the gods inherit. Beneath is all the fiend's. . . " (177–178; *King Lear* 4.6.112–113, 122–131). However, by the end of the novel, John, like the characters in Shakespeare's play, recognizes that in spite of human wickedness and suffering, "the gods are just and of our pleasant vices make instruments to plague us" (211; *King Lear* 5.3.173–177). Even if the gods sometimes seem malignant ("As flies to wanton boys are we to the gods; they kill us for their sport"), they are really "ever-gentle gods" (226; *King Lear* 4.1.36–37 and 4.6.219). *King Lear*, then, shows not only how people lash out at those who have wronged them but also how they become reconciled to imperfect life by understanding that moral order prevails.

Huxley's knowledge of Shakespeare is vast. Besides these seven plays, he has John quote from *Antony and Cleopatra*, *As You Like It*, *Julius Caesar*, *King John*, *Measure for Measure*, *Timon of Athens*, *Twelfth Night*, and the poem "The Phoenix and the Turtle." All of these references add richness to the novel as Huxley uses Shakespeare's plays to illustrate the powerful passions that the world state is dedicated to eradicating. Shakespeare's beautiful words are also used to contrast with the silly jingles repeated by the Brave New World people. Through John, readers come to understand that knowledge of Shakespeare, and, therefore, knowledge of the arts and humanities, enrich people's lives.

Literary Reception of the Novel

When *Brave New World* appeared in February 1932, it was a huge financial success. English readers eagerly bought 13,000 copies in 1932 and 10,000 the next year. However, Americans were not as excited, finding the book too pessimistic; fewer than 3,000 copies sold in the United States during its first year (Bedford, 251).

In spite of its popular appeal in Great Britain, most literary reviewers did not enthusiastically embrace Huxley's work. They disapproved of it both as a work of art, finding it "weak in plot and characterization, shallow, mechanical in structure, and monotonous in tone," and also as a book of prophecy because "they did not find his point relevant, insightful, alarming, or particularly original." The British reviewer for *New Statesman* and *Nation* was extremely harsh, condemning the novel as "a thin little joke" that "lacks in richness" because "we want rather more of a prophecy than Mr. Huxley gives us." He complained that even though "there are brilliant, sardonic little splinters of hate," Huxley has nothing new to offer but instead "elaborates conjectures and opinions already familiar to readers of his essays. . . . There are not surprises in it; and if he had no surprises to give us, why should Mr. Huxley have bothered to turn this essay in indignation into a novel?" This reviewer felt that "Nothing can bring it alive" (quoted in "Too Far Ahead," 7–8).

Some reviewers, such as London's *Times Literary Supplement* critic, found the book boring because "it is not easy to become interested in the scientifically imagined details of life in this mechanical Utopia." He was also dismayed by the amount of sexuality found in the book, adding, "Nor is there compensation in the amount of attention that he gives to the abundant sex life of these denatured human beings" (quoted in "Too Far Ahead", 8).

In America, Granville Hicks of the Communist Party USA blasted the book in the *New Republic* for being politically inappropriate because it failed to examine the topics Hicks believed were the most important issues of the 1930s—the "war in Asia, bankruptcy in Europe, and starvation everywhere." He attacked Huxley personally because he "has money, social position, talent, friends, prestige, and he is effectively insulated from the misery of the masses. Of course he wants something to worry about, even if he has to go a long, long way to find it" (quoted in "Too Far Ahead", 8–9).

Of course, not all professional critics were negative. For example, the *New York Times* reviewer found Huxley's novel an entertaining satire but not a work to be taken as a serious warning for the future, writing that "it is a little difficult to take alarm" since it would only take "one Rousseau to shake [the mechanized world] to the foundations" (Chamberlain, 54–55). Like the *Times*, the *Nation* also found the work "successful as a novel and as a satire" but did not think that "Mr. Huxley's central problem" would "become a real problem" based on the amount of suffering and chaos in the world (Hazlitt, 53).

Although literary critics did not find Huxley's issues relevant, the famous American author Edith Wharton was very taken with the book, calling it "a masterpiece of tragic indictment of our ghastly age of Fordian culture" (quoted in Murray, 257). A leading biologist was also enthralled by "Mr. Huxley's remarkable book," writing in 1932, "Unfortunately, what gives the biologist a sardonic smile as he reads it, is the fact that *the biology is perfectly right*, and Mr. Huxley has included nothing in his book but what might be regarded as legitimate extrapolations from knowledge and power that we already have." This biologist recommended that the book be required reading for those "who suppose that science alone can be the saviour [*sic*] of the world" and felt that "humanity . . . will always owe great debt" to Huxley for pointing out the problems of the present (Needham, 59–60).

In subsequent decades, very few literary critics have analyzed Huxley's most famous novel. However, those who have written about *Brave New World* have been mostly positive. For example, Harold H. Watts, writing in 1969, found *Brave New World* to be an "esthetic success" and admired it as "a work that expresses the twentieth-century cultural situation" (83–84). A twenty-first century critic, although detesting "laconic old Aldous" Huxley's "didactic and pedagogic and faintly superior" tone, recognizes that Huxley's book has value for present-day readers because it shows "the splendors and miseries, not just of modernity, but of the human condition" (Hitchens, viii, xi, xx).

Even though most literary scholars have disregarded *Brave New World*, they recognize the novel's importance as one of the greatest anti-utopian novels and as a leader in the science fiction genre. In 1962 one critic called it the "archetypal dystopia" (Walsh, 112), and in 1963 it was looked upon as the "most influential anti-utopian novel of the twentieth century" (Kateb, 126). By 1986 it was recognized as "arguably the Western world's most famous science fiction novel" (Aldiss and Wingrove, 184).

In spite of the novel's popularity with readers, a number of censors have found *Brave New World* a dangerous work because of its promotion of drugs, sexual promiscuity, and suicide, as well as its antireligious and antifamily sentiments. It was immediately banned in Ireland in 1932. Beginning in the 1980s, it has been frequently challenged in America. In 1980 it was removed from a classroom in Miller, Missouri. Eight years later it was questioned as required reading at a high school in Yukon, Oklahoma, because of its "language and moral content" (Doyle, 57, no. 665), and in 1993, the Corona-Norco, California, unified school district felt that it "centered around negative activity" and unsuccessfully challenged it (Doyle, 57, no. 665). However, in 2000, it was successfully challenged and removed from the Foley, Alabama, high school library when a parent "complained that its characters showed contempt for religion, marriage and the family" (Doyle, 57, no. 665). As recently as 2003, parents in the South Texas Independent School District in Mercedes, Texas, "objected to the adult themes—sexuality, drugs, and suicide" (Doyle, 57, no. 665). Although the school board did not remove the book, it did require principals to offer an alternative to a challenged book.

Unlike the censors who wish to ban *Brave New World* and unlike the literary scholars who have basically ignored Huxley's novel, twenty-first-century readers are still gripped by Huxley's anti-utopian book. One reader says that, after reading *Brave New World*, "I got . . . the sense of the predicament of the individual in a world of manufactured sameness. I felt for the first time the possibility of man as an ultimately self-destructive force devouring and denying the natural world, I saw the alienation that leads to planetary suicide. This is the name of our song as we approach the third millennium. This is where Aldous Huxley functioned as a prophet and can be of great help now to those who come upon him for the first time" (McKenna, xii).

Aside from *Brave New World*, Huxley's book-length essays, *The Doors of Perception* and *Heaven and Hell*, established him as a psychedelic guru of the 1960s counterculture.

Chapter 4

Huxley's Place in Literature

BY THE TIME ALDOUS HUXLEY wrote his fifth novel, *Brave New World*, he was "the preeminent figure in the vanguard of English intellectual and literary culture. His name alone conveyed a mood of ironic social and literary criticism, reflecting his talent for propounding shocking new ideas while attacking works and theories he considered hopelessly outdated" (Sisk, 122). His early biting, satirical novels, including *Crome Yellow*, *Antic Hay*, *Those Barren Leaves*, and *Point Counter Point*, were well received by many of the cynical post–World War I crowd, although, in the mid-1930s, "librarians were still ready to ban his books in some places and the stock attitude of reviewers was to label Huxley 'Intellectual—slightly unpleasant'" (Murray, 278). However, almost everyone agreed that Huxley was a brilliant writer, and the public embraced *Brave New World* when it was published in 1932. It has remained popular since that time, but not always for reasons Huxley would approve of. For example, "it is said to have been popular with American college students in the 1950s because of its picture of apparently unlimited and guiltless sexual freedom" (Murray, 257). No matter what the reason, *Brave New World* has remained Huxley's best-loved work.

As a result of this one triumphant book, many people are unaware that Huxley was a prolific writer, producing almost fifty books during his long career. He wrote in a variety of styles, including novels, essays, short stories, biographies, poetry, travelogues, and drama. After *Brave New World*, Huxley's book-length essay, *The Doors of Perception*, is probably his best-known book. It became extremely popular in the 1960s as the cult book for hippies and others who used psychedelic drugs. The 1960s and 1970s rock band The Doors, famous for its acid-trip-influenced music, took its name from Huxley's book, and the Beatles, inspired by Huxley's ideas, placed a picture of him on the sleeve of their 1967 album, "Sgt. Pepper's Lonely Hearts Club Band."

Since there are some questionable reasons for the popularity of some of Huxley's books, it is not too surprising

A decade after his death, Aldous Huxley remained such a fixture of pop culture that he made the cover of the Beatle's album, "Sgt. Pepper's Lonely Hearts Club Band."

that several of his works have been banned or challenged as acceptable reading material. As might be expected, *Brave New World* has been the work most often challenged because of its explicit discussion of sex, the use of drugs, and suicide. But other Huxley books have also been considered dangerous. Ireland banned *Eyeless in Gaza* from 1926 to 1953, and *Point Counter Point,* in 1930, finding it offensive to public morals (Doyle, 58, numbers 667, 668). *Antic Hay* found disfavor in the United States. In Boston, Massachusetts, it was banned in 1930 because of obscenity, and in 1952 in Baltimore, Maryland, a teacher was fired for assigning this novel to a senior literature class (Doyle, 57, number 664). *The Doors of Perception* was challenged by the Oconto, Wisconsin, Unified School District in 1980 because it "glorifies the use of drugs" (Doyle, 58, number 666).

In spite of the protests to some of his works, Huxley, throughout his life, was recognized as a leading author. He received three major awards from the literary community. In 1939 he was given the James Tait Black Memorial Prize, Scotland's most prestigious and the United Kingdom's oldest literary award, for *After Many a Summer Dies the Swan*. In the United States, the American Academy of Arts and Letters honored Huxley in 1959 with the Award of Merit for the Novel. Three years later, he was elected Companion of Literature by the Royal Society of Literature.

Curiously, critics have not responded to Huxley in the same way as readers and the literary community, who particularly admire *Brave New World*. Literary critics have basically disregarded his novels and have published very few critical books on Huxley's works; almost nothing has appeared in recent years. There are three recent collections of essays on *Brave New World*, those by Katie De Koster (1999), Harold Bloom (2003), and David Garrett Izzo and Kim Kirkpatrick (2008), but most of the essays in these books are old. Huxley's life has not been of much interest to biographers. The earliest and most complete biography, written by Huxley's friend Sybille Bedford, was first published in 1973. Nearly thirty years later, in 2002, two biographies appeared, one by Nicholas Murray, which looks at Huxley's relationships with other people, and the second by Dana Sawyer, which examines Huxley's life and philosophy.

Although the professional critics continue to ignore Huxley's works, the public does not. Many people continue to enjoy his books, particularly *Brave New World*, the novel with the most prestige in both the twentieth and the twenty-first centuries. Since its publication, it has been influential as a science fiction novel and as the model for anti-utopian literature. Writing in 1993, John Clute, the editor of *The Encyclopedia of Science Fiction*, claimed that "*Brave New World* remains a central work" of the science fiction genre because Huxley "used the devices of SF [science fiction] to host, and to grapple with, the nightmare of history during a century . . . of change and of nightmares about the end of change" in order to examine "the profoundest fear" of serious science fiction writers "that somehow the world will suddenly stop shifting at the wrong moment, locking us into a malign stasis." It is the fear of "fixity" that is the "terror at the heart of *Brave New World* . . . [which] closes with the suicide of Mr Savage, the only character capable of reflecting our humane nostalgia for rounded human beings alive in a supple world." This dread of a changeless, destructive future which Huxley so skillfully demonstrates in *Brave New World* is, Clute explained, "the true science fiction impulse" (Clute, 93–94). Huxley's prophetic novel is one of the most influential science fiction books of the twentieth century.

Of even more importance than its influence in the science fiction genre is the novel's wide sphere of influence as a philosophical document. People in a variety of fields have come to recognize that many of the issues Huxley raised in his anti-utopian novel have come to pass, and numerous writers have modified and expanded Huxley's ideas to discuss a number of current issues. Scientists, social and political analysts, philosophers, theologians, techies, and historians use the words *Brave New World* in their book titles to show that they are dealing with issues related to modern scientific advances and their effects on human beings. This appropriation of a novel's title is almost unprecedented; as biographer Murray exclaims, it "has become the stuff of journalistic clichés" (256).

Scientists concerned with advances in biology, particularly biotechnology and genetics, have used the phrase *Brave New World* in their book titles, as Michael W. Fox did in *Superpigs and Wondercorn: The Brave New World of Biotechnology and Where It All May Lead* and Lee M. Silver did in *Remaking Eden: Cloning and Beyond in a Brave New World.*

Those concerned with social issues also adopt Huxley's title. People can read about *The Brave New World of Health Care*, *Psychochemistry*, *American Sex*, *Work*, *America's Fiscal Future*, and even the *Monarch Butterfly*. And they can learn about a *Brave New Wealthy World* and *Brave New Stepfamilies.*

Political writers borrow the words *Brave New World*, discussing topics such as terrorism, national defense, oil prices, and treaties in books like Wladyslaw Pleszczynski's *Our Brave New World*: *Essays on the Impact of September 11* and Julian West's *Just Another Brave New World? Oil Companies and Iraq*.

Analysts looking at problems in various countries have taken their titles from Huxley's novel. The Soviet Union, China, South Africa, Japan, the United States, Uruguay, Australia, Tanzania, and Europe have all been examined as types of *Brave New Worlds* in areas such as opium wars, apartheid, domestic politics, foreign policies, international trading, marketing, and trade unions.

Techies interested in the Internet or computers draw on Huxley's title. Two of these books are Grant Fjermedal's *Tomorrow Makers: A Brave New World of Living-Brain Machines* and Alex Lightman's *Brave New Unwired World: The Digital Big Bang and the Infinite Internet.*

Theologians and philosophers adopt Huxley's title, too. John S. and Paul D. Feinberg's *Ethics for a Brave New World* and Joni Eareckson Tada and Nigel M. de. S. Cameron's *How to be a Christian in a Brave New World* are two books examining ethics and theology.

In the field of law, there is a book that teaches lawyers how to proactively bring about change, Leonard M. Salter's *Law as a Lever: Building a Brave New World*, and there are a number of books that discuss the ethical use of law on a variety of topics—bioethics, health care, entertainers' rights, immigration policies, and medical malpractice. The Pennsylvania Bar Institute has published two of these works: *Healthcare Joint Ventures: The Brave New World* and *Brave New World of Medical Malpractice Litigation.*

Historians such as Louis I. Bredvold in *Brave New World of the Enlightenment* and Peter Charles Hoffer in *Brave New World: A History of Early America* talk about the *Brave New World* of the past.

Huxley's title has even been transformed from *World* to *Universe* in Paul Halpern and Paul Wessons's *Brave New Universe: Illuminating the Darkest Secrets of the Cosmos.*

Of these many types of books that look at issues raised by Huxley's *Brave New World*, three-fourths of them have appeared in the last two decades, with the majority of them being published in the twenty-first century. As the world advances in scientific and technological expertise, Huxley's predictions and warnings seem to be more pressing.

In popular culture, Huxley's *Brave New World* has also found a solid niche. The book's title has been used for an art exhibition catalog, a dictionary, a book of cartoons, and a comics institute. Artists have written their own versions of Huxley's book. For example, poet Archibald MacLeish wrote a poem entitled *Brave New World*, and various rock musicians and bands, including Iron Maiden, have composed albums called *Brave New World*. In television, the novel has served as the inspiration and title of episodes on several shows, including *seaQuest 2032*, *7th Heaven*, and *Facts of Life*. In addition, there have been two television movies made of *Brave New World*, one in 1980 and one in 1998. Overall, Huxley's anti-utopian novel has had a huge impact on American culture.

Huxley's fame and relevance in the twenty-first century rests almost exclusively on *Brave New World*, a book biographer Nicholas Murray is convinced will continue to be important in this new century. He writes: "When college syllabi and newspaper lists of the best of most highly regarded books of the twentieth century are drawn up, it will always find a place" (256). The novel is not only significant as a prototype of science fiction novels that are so popular today, but, it is also important because its issues remain pertinent, especially its warnings that people may lose their humanity. In the twenty-first century, a time when citizens admirably strive to create a better, more sensitive, and more equal world, there is the danger of losing freedom and individuality as everyone is pressured to conform to societal ideals—to be politically correct, to get along with others at all costs, and to believe that everyone is equal and, therefore, the same. As critic William Matter points out, Huxley's novel "warns the reader that 'perfection' of the state entails absolute social stability, and social stability entails the effacement of personal freedom" (61). Huxley's novel presents a clear picture that total conformity results in loss of individuality, true humanity, and meaningful life, which are all issues that concern those living in the twenty-first century.

Works

Novels

1921 *Crome Yellow*
1923 *Antic Hay*
1925 *Those Barren Leaves*
1928 *Point Counter Point*
1932 *Brave New World*
1936 *Eyeless in Gaza*
1939 *After Many a Summer Dies the Swan*
1944 *Time Must Have a Stop*
1948 *Ape and Essence*
1955 *The Genius and the Goddess*
1962 *Island*

Books of Essays

1923 *On the Margin*
1925 *Along the Road*
1926 *Essays New and Old* (U.S. title *Essays Old and New*)
1927 *Proper Studies*
1929 *Do What You Will*
1930 *Vulgarity in Literature*
1931 *Music at Night*
1932 *Texts and Pretexts*
1936 *The Olive Tree*
1936 *What Are You Going to Do About It?*
1937 *Ends and Means*
1942 *The Art of Seeing*
1945 *The Perennial Philosophy*

1946 *Science, Liberty and Peace*
1950 *Themes and Variations*
1954 *The Doors of Perception*
1956 *Heaven and Hell*
1956 *Adonis and the Alphabet* (U.S. title *Tomorrow and Tomorrow and Tomorrow*)
1958 *Brave New World Revisited*
1963 *Literature and Science*
1977 *The Human Situation* (published posthumously)

Books of Short Stories

1920 *Limbo*
1922 *Mortal Coils*
1924 *Little Mexican*
1926 *Two or Three Graces*
1930 *Brief Candles*

Biography

1941 *Gray Eminence*
1952 *The Devils of Loudun*

Poetry

1916 *The Burning Wheel*
1917 *Jonah*
1918 *The Defeat of Youth*
1920 *Leda*
1931 *The Cicadas*

Travel

1926 *Jesting Pilate*
1934 *Beyond the Mexique Bay*

Drama

1931 *The World of Light*
1948 *The Gioconda Smile*

Filmography

1998 *Brave New World*. USA Television Network movie. Directed by Leslie Libman and Larry Williams. Starring Peter Gallagher and Leonard Nimoy. Universal TV.

1996 *Aldous Huxley: The Gravity of Light*. Video. Directed by Oliver Hockenhull. Cinéma Esperança International Inc.

1994 *Aldous Huxley: Darkness and Light*. Video. Directed by Chris Hunt. BBC.

1980 *Brave New World*. USA Television Network movie. Directed by Burt Brinckerhoff. Starring Bud Cort and Marcia Strassman. Universal TV.

Chronology

1894	
July 26:	Aldous Leonard Huxley, the third son, after Julian and Trevenen, of Leonard and Julia Arnold Huxley, is born at Godalming, Surrey, England.
1899	Huxley's sister, Margaret, is born.
1902	
January 23:	Julia Huxley opens a school for girls at Prior's Field.
1903	
Autumn:	Huxley attends Preparatory School at Hillside.
1908	
September:	Huxley enters Eton College, planning to specialize in biology.
November 29:	Huxley's mother dies.
1911	
March:	Huxley leaves Eton because of an attack of severe inflammation of the eyes, which causes near blindness.
1912	
February 23:	Huxley's father marries Rosalind Bruce.
April:	Huxley's sight begins to improve.

May–June: Huxley studies German and music in Marburg, Germany.

1913

October: Huxley enters Balliol College, Oxford.

1914

August 23: Huxley's brother, Trevenen, age 24, commits suicide.

1915

December: Huxley first visits Garsington, home of Philip and Lady Ottoline Morrell.

1916

January: Huxley is rejected by the army as unfit for service.

June: Huxley takes school examinations, receiving a First in English literature and winning the Stanhope Historical Essay Prize.

September: *The Burning Wheel*, Huxley's first volume of poetry, is published. Huxley begins living at Garsington, working on Philip Morrell's farm.

1917

September 18: Huxley becomes a schoolmaster at Eton.

December: *Jonah* is published.

1918

August: *The Defeat of Youth, and Other Poems* is published.

1919

April: Huxley joins the editorial staff of the *Athenaeum* in London.

July 10: Huxley marries Maria Nys.

1920

February: *Limbo* is published.

April 19: Son, Matthew Huxley, is born.

May: *Leda* is published.

October: Huxley works for Condé Nast on the staff of *House and Garden*.

1921

November: *Crome Yellow,* Huxley's first novel, is published.

1922

May: *Mortal Coils*, a collection of stories, is published.

1923

May: *On the Margin* is published.

November: *Antic Hay* is published.

1924

May: *Little Mexican* is published.

September: Huxley begins traveling in Italy, Holland, Belgium, and France.

1925

January: *Those Barren Leaves* is published.

September: *Along the Road* is published. Huxley and Maria begin a round-the-world trip.

1926

May: *Two or Three Graces* is published.

October: *Jesting Pilate* is published. Huxley renews friendship with D. H. Lawrence and his wife.

December: *Essays New and Old* (U.S. title *Essays Old and New*) is published.

1927
November: *Proper Studies* is published.

1928
June: Huxley and Maria move to France.
November: *Point Counter Point* is published.

1929
October: *Do What You Will* is published.

1930
May: *Brief Candles* is published.
November: *Vulgarity in Literature* is published.

1931
May: *The Cicadas* is published.
September: *Music at Night* is published.

1932
February: *Brave New World* is published.
September: *The Letters of D. H. Lawrence*, edited by Aldous Huxley, is published.
November: *Texts and Pretexts* is published.

1933
January–May: Huxley and Maria travel in the West Indies, Guatemala, and Mexico.
May 3: Huxley's father dies.

1934
April: *Beyond the Mexique Bay* is published.
December: The Huxleys move to Albany, Piccadilly, England.

1935 Huxley becomes active in the pacifist movement.

1936

April: *What Are You Going To Do About It?*, a peace pamphlet, is published.

June: *Eyeless in Gaza* is published.

December: *The Olive Tree* is published.

1937

April 7: Huxley, Maria, and Matthew travel to the United States to begin continental tour.

November: *Ends and Means* published.

November–December: Huxley and Gerald Heard lecture on peace throughout the United States.

1938

February: The Huxleys move to Los Angeles, California.

August-September: Huxley works for Metro-Goldwyn-Mayer on a script of *Madame Curie*.

November: Huxley attempts to improve his sight by the Bates Method.

1939

August: Huxley works on an adaptation of *Pride and Prejudice* for MGM.

October: *After Many a Summer Dies the Swan* is published.

1941

October: *Grey Eminence* is published.

1942

March: Huxley works at Twentieth Century Fox on *Jane Eyre*.

October: *The Art of Seeing* is published.

1944
August: *Time Must Have a Stop* is published.

1945
September: *The Perennial Philosophy* is published.
November–
December: Huxley works with Walt Disney on film of *Alice in Wonderland.*

1946
March: *Science, Liberty and Peace* is published.

1948
February: *Mortal Coils* (later called *The Gioconda Smile*), a play, is published.
August: *Ape and Essence* is published.

1950
April: *Themes and Variations* is published. Son Matthew marries Ellen Hovde.

1951
October 20: Huxley's grandson, Mark Trevenen, is born.

1952
January: Maria becomes seriously ill.
October: *The Devils of Loudun* is published.

1953
May: Huxley first takes the hallucinogenic drug mescaline under a doctor's supervision.
October: Huxley's granddaughter, Tessa, is born.

1954

February: *The Doors of Perception* is published.

April-August: Huxley and Maria tour France, the Near East, Cyprus, Greece, Italy, and England.

1955

February 12: Maria Huxley dies.

June: *The Genius and the Goddess* is published.

1956

February: *Heaven and Hell* is published.

March 19: Huxley marries Laura Archera.

October: *Adonis and the Alphabet* (U.S. title *Tomorrow and Tomorrow and Tomorrow*) is published.

1958

July–December: Huxley and Laura travel in Peru, Brazil, Italy, England, and France.

October: *Brave New World Revisited* is published.

1959

February–May: Huxley is a visiting professor at the University of California at Santa Barbara. He receives the Award of Merit for the Novel from the American Academy of Arts and Letters.

1960

March–April: Huxley is a visiting professor at the Menninger Foundation in Topeka, Kansas.

April–May: Huxley presents a series of lectures called "What a Piece of Work Is Man."

May–July: Huxley is diagnosed with cancer of the tongue and receives radiation treatment.

September: Huxley receives an honorary degree from the University of New Hampshire.

September–November: Huxley is a visiting professor at Massachusetts Institute of Technology.

1961

May 12: Huxley's house is destroyed by fire, and Huxley loses his library and all his papers.

1962

February–May: Huxley is a visiting professor at Berkeley.

March: *Island* is published.

June: Huxley is elected Companion of Literature by the Royal Society of Literature.

June–July: Huxley's cancer recurs; he has an operation followed by cobalt treatment.

August–September: Huxley attends a meeting of the World Academy of Arts and Sciences in Brussels.

November: Huxley lectures in the Middle West and East Coast of the United States.

1963

March–April: Huxley lectures at Oregon, Berkeley, and Stanford.

April–July: Huxley has another relapse of cancer and receives radiation treatment.

August: Huxley goes to Stockholm for a meeting of the World Academy of Arts and Sciences.

September: *Literature and Science* is published.
Fall: Huxley composes "Shakespeare and Religion" on his deathbed.
November 22: Huxley dies in Los Angeles; his body is cremated. There is no funeral service.
December 17: A memorial service is held in London at Friends' House.

1971
October 27: Huxley's ashes are buried in his parents' grave at Compton, Surrey, England.

1972
October 10: Maria Huxley's ashes are buried by the side of Huxley.

1977 *The Human Situation* is published posthumously.

Notes

Chapter 1

p. 10, par. 3, At a memorial gathering held a few weeks after his death, friends and family met to remember Huxley. For his brother, Huxley's fundamental characteristics were "gentleness" and "essential goodness" (Julian Huxley, [Tribute], 23). For his sister-in-law, he possessed "gentleness and depth" (Juliette Huxley, 40). Dr. Osmond called him "wise and gentle," filled with "kindness and tolerance" (Osmond 122, 116). A college classmate remembered him primarily for the "profound sweetness of his character" (Mortimer, 137). Fellow writers found him "gentle and lovable" (Eliot, 32), "charitable and good" (Spender, 20), a man of "essential gentleness and sweetness" (Woolf, 35) who had an "air of general benevolence" and "seemed never to be angry" (Sitwell, 33). Citations from Julian Huxley, ed. *Aldous Huxley: 1894–1963: A Memorial Volume* (New York: Harper & Row, 1965).

p. 21, par. 3, Biographer Nicholas Murray writes a detailed description of the complicated relationship between Huxley, Maria, and Mary Hutchinson. See *Aldous Huxley: A Biography* (New York: St. Martin's Press, 2002), 143–145, 153–154, 165, 188, 190, 203, 214, 220.

Chapter 2

p. 38, par. 1, For more information on the scientific advances taking place at the end of the nineteenth and the beginning of the twentieth century, see Rebecca Fraser, *The Story of Britain: From the Romans to the Present: A*

Narrative History (New York: W. W. Norton, 2005), 625–632; John Peck and Martin Coyle, *A Brief History of English Literature* (Hampshire, England: Palgrave, 2002), 322–323; and Dana Sawyer, *Aldous Huxley: A Biography* (New York: The Crossroad Publishing Company, 2002), 39–41.

p. 50, par. 2, In *Ape and Essence*, Huxley censures the world community for letting World War II take place, explaining that people let themselves be filled with the devil: "The Belial in them wanted the Communist Revolution, wanted the Fascist reaction to that revolution, wanted Mussolini and Hitler and the Politburo, wanted famine, inflation and depression; wanted armaments as a cure for unemployment; wanted the persecution of the Jews and the Kulaks; wanted the Nazis and the Communists to divide Poland and then go to war with one another. . . . He wanted concentration camps and gas chambers and cremation ovens. He wanted saturation bombing." *Ape and Essence* (New York: Harper & Brothers, 1948), 129.

Chapter 3

p. 61, par. 1, Quite understandably, H. G. Wells was not happy with Huxley's attack, telling a critic, "*Brave New World* was a great disappointment to me. A writer of the standing of Aldous Huxley has no right to betray the future as he did in that book. When thinking about the future, people seem to overlook the logical progress in education, in architecture, and science." Quoted in Peter Firchow, *Aldous Huxley: Satirist and Novelist* (Minneapolis: University of Minnesota Press, 1972), 120.

p. 64, par. 3, All quotations are taken from Aldous Huxley, *Brave New World and Brave New World Revisited*, foreword by Christopher Hitchens (New York: Harper Perennial, 2005). All quotations to *Brave New World* are from this edition and are cited in the text.

p. 68, par. 2, Huxley's motto, "Community, Identity, Stability," mimics the slogan of the eighteenth-century Jacobins, the French revolutionaries who instituted the Reign of Terror. These ancestors of Soviet communism had the motto: "Liberty, equality, fraternity."

p. 78, par. 1, Huxley's new society began in 1908 with the introduction of Ford's Model T. In A.F. 141 (A.D. 2049), the "Nine Years' War" broke out (52); this was a time of Russian ecological warfare, including anthrax bombing and poisoning water supplies (53). The war brought about the "great Economic Collapse" (53), and "World Control" began in A.F. 150 (A.D. 2058) (56). During the next centuries, the social instability continued, but, with the discovery of soma and the developments in science and technology, the "ideal" world state was in existence by A.F. 632 (A.D. 2540), the time of *Brave New World*. For a timeline of the events leading to the World Control, see Robert S. Baker, "History and Psychology in the World State: Chapter 3," in Harold Bloom, ed., *Aldous Huxley's "Brave New World"* (Philadelphia: Chelsea House Publishers, 2003), 121–122.

p. 80, par. 2. For more information on the structure of the novel, see Keith M. May, *Aldous Huxley* (New York: Barnes and Noble Books, 1972), 100–117.

p. 84, par. 1, "Georgie Porgie" is a nursery rhyme about a boy who kisses girls who do not want to be kissed. Since he is afraid the other boys will punish him, he runs away when the boys appear. "Georgie Porgie pudding and pie, / Kissed the girls and made them cry. / When the boys came out to play, / Georgie Porgie ran away."

p. 85, par. 4, Huxley satirizes other political leaders. Hoover's secretary of the treasury during the stock-market collapse, Andrew Mellon, and the Spanish dictator Primo de Rivera become the newspaper reporter Primo Mellon. Habibullah Khan, the progressive leader of Afghanistan from 1901 until 1919, who attempted to bring Western medicine and other modern technology to Afghanistan, becomes Lenina's date, Jean-Jacques Habibullah. Sarojini Naidu, a female political activist and Indian poet whom Huxley admired, becomes Sarojini Engels, a Solidarity Service participant. Charles Bradlaugh, an English political activist and atheist, turns into Fifi Bradlaugh, another Solidarity Service participant. Popé, an Indian American rebel, is Linda's rebellious lover.

p. 86, par. 1, Huxley lampoons other capitalists and technological leaders as well. Ford's son, Edsel, appears as George Edzel, one of the Alpha boys. Conformist Henry Foster may be named for William Foster, head of a British company that made agricultural machinery and built the first tanks for the British Army in World War I, or he may be identified with William Z. Foster, an American labor agitator and Communist leader. Huxley's scientist Pilkington gets his name from a nineteenth-century glass-manufacturing company (which is still in business). Several of the names of the Solidarity Service attendees are derived from capitalist leaders, including Joanna Diesel (from the German inventor Rudolf Diesel, who invented the diesel engine in 1898), Clara Deterding (from Henri Deterding, who was one of the founders of the Royal Dutch Petroleum Company), and the repulsive, one-eyebrowed Morgana Rothschild (from two successful bankers, J. P. Morgan, an American, and the Rothschild family, a famous European banking dynasty).

p. 86, par. 2, Huxley thought that people were too enthralled with Freud. Psychiatrist Humphry Osmond tells a humorous story about taking Huxley to a conference of the American Psychiatric Association in the 1950s: "He sat there paying the keenest attention, crossing himself devoutly every time Freud's name was mentioned. In *Brave New World*, the Saviour was called 'Our Ford', or as certain people for some unexplained reason preferred to call him, 'Our Freud'. Here was a congregation, including many pious Freudians, so Aldous was kept busy. Luckily my psychiatric colleagues were so absorbed by the incantations that no one noticed him." [Tribute], in Julian Huxley, *Aldous Huxley*, 118.

p. 87, par. 2, Another socially prominent man, Ekai Kawaguchi, a Japanese Buddhist monk, appears twice in *Brave New World*. Huxley calls a scientist "Kawaguchi" and a Solidarity Service participant "Tom Kawaguchi."

p. 88, par. 1, Huxley also includes Solomon J. Rubinowitz, an American Yiddish author whose tales of ordinary Russian Jews became the basis for the popular musical *Fiddler on the Roof*. Huxley gives his name to Reuben Rabinovitch, the little boy who taught the Fordian society the possibilities of sleep-teaching common people.

p. 88, par. 2, For more discussion on Huxley's use of names, see David W. Sisk, "Using Language in a World That Debases Language," in Katie de Koster, ed., *Readings on "Brave New World"* (San Diego: Greenhaven Press, 1999), 122–129.

p. 91, par. 2, According to Peter Edgerly Firchow, Huxley uses *The Tempest* to hint "at the analogy between the Fordian state and Prospero's island" in order "to convey ironically a disapproval of that state without ever having to voice it himself." He demonstrates the various ways a reader can ironically view the characters: "Mond is Prospero; Lenina is Miranda; the Savage is Ferdinand; Bernard Marx is Caliban. Or, if one prefers, Mond is a kind of Prospero and Alonso combined; the Savage, as befits his name, is Caliban, and his mother Linda, is Sycorax; Lenina is a perverse Miranda and Bernard a strange Ferdinand." "The End of Utopia: A Study of Aldous Huxley's *Brave New World*," in Bloom, *Aldous Huxley's "Brave New World,"* 107.

p. 96, par. 1, Huxley uses a number of short quotes from Shakespeare's plays. *Antony and Cleopatra* provides a statement about death: "Eternity was in our lips and eyes" (143; *Antony and Cleopatra,* 1.3.35). John uses the words from *As You Like It* to describe the way the Fordian citizens behave as babies "mewling and puking" (192; *As You Like It*, 2.7.143). When he wants to give a public speech, John borrows Mark Antony's words in *Julius Caesar*, "Lend me your ears" (191; *Julius Caesar*, 3.2.75). The Savage recognizes the religious term *cardinal* when the Controller uses it and quotes from *King John*: "I Pandulph, of fair Milan, cardinal" (208; *King John,* 3.1.138). When ruminating about the relationship between sleep and death, John adds words from *Measure for Measure*: "thy best of rest is sleep and that thou oft provok'st; yet grossly fear'st thy death which is no more" (226–227; *Measure for Measure* 3.1.17–19). Looking at Lenina's half-naked body, John is reminded of a line from *Timon of Athens*: "For those milk paps that through the window bars bore at men's eyes" (175; *Timon of Athens*, 4.3.118–119). John affirms that he is the one speaking on the phone by quoting from *Twelfth Night*, "If I do not usurp myself, I am" (179; *Twelfth Night,* 1.5.182). John reads portions of Shakespeare's poem "The Phoenix and the Turtle" to Helmholtz: "Let the bird of loudest lay / On the sole Arabian tree, / Herald sad and trumpet be. . . . / Property was thus appall'd, / That the self was not the same; / Single nature's double name / Neither two nor one was call'd / Reason in itself confounded / Saw division grow together" (167; "The Phoenix and the Turtle," lines 1–3, 37–42).

Chapter 4

p. 106, par. 6, For a more comprehensive list of the books bearing the title *Brave New World*, see the bibliography.
p. 107, par. 1, The art exhibition catalog is *Brave New World of Fritz Brandtner* by Helen Duffy and Frances K. Smith. The dictionary is *More Brave New Words: The Latest, Funniest, and Most Original Dictionary in the World* by Bill Sherk. The book of cartoons is *Dahl's Brave New World* by Francis W. Dahl. The comics institute, *Brave New World Institute*, is located in California.

Further Information

Further Reading

Barfoot, C. C., ed. *Aldous Huxley between East and West*. New York: Rodopi, 2001.

Bedford, Sybille. *Aldous Huxley: A Biography.* New York: Harper & Row, 1974.

Birnbaum, Milton. *Aldous Huxley: A Quest for Values.* New Brunswick, NJ: Transaction Publishers, 2006.

Bloom, Harold, ed. *Aldous Huxley*. Philadelphia: Chelsea House, 2003.

———, ed. *Aldous Huxley's "Brave New World."* Philadelphia: Chelsea House Publishers, 2003.

Huxley, Laura Archera. *This Timeless Moment: A Personal View of Aldous Huxley*. Berkeley, CA: Celestial Arts, 2000.

Izzo, David Garrett, and Kim Kirkpatrick, eds. *Huxley's "Brave New World": Essays*. Jefferson, NC: McFarland and Coy, 2008.

Murray, Nicholas. *Aldous Huxley: A Biography.* New York: St. Martin's Press, 2002.

Sawyer, Dana. *Aldous Huxley: A Biography*. New York: The Crossroad Publishing Company, 2002.

Web Sites

http://www.anglistik.uni-muenster.de/Huxley/
The Centre for Aldous Huxley Studies website by the University of Münster in Germany includes news and events of the Aldous Huxley Society as well as information about the Huxley library and the Huxley annual publication.

http://www.huxley.net/index.html
David Pearce's website includes essays on Huxley's works as well as a full online text of *Brave New World*. This site also includes video clips of a 1962 interview with Huxley.

http://www.imdb.com/name/nm0404717/
The Internet Movie Database's page on Huxley includes a biography and a filmography.

http://www.litweb.net/biography/266/Aldous_Huxley.html
This site offers biographical information as well as a list of works by Huxley.

http://www.online-literature.com/aldous_huxley/
The Literature Network website includes a biography and a searchable collection of works. This site also includes an online literature forum.

http://www.somaweb.org/
This site contains biographical information, list of works, a discussion forum, and additional links.

Bibliography

Primary Sources

Huxley, Aldous. *Ape and Essence.* New York: Harper & Brothers, 1948.

———. *Brave New World* and *Brave New World Revisited.* Foreword by Christopher Hitchens. New York: Harper Perennial, 2005.

———. *Island.* New York: Harper & Brothers, 1962.

———. *Letters of Aldous Huxley.* Ed. Grover Smith. New York: Harper & Row, 1969.

———. "Preface." *Brave New World* and *Brave New World Revisited.* Foreword by Christopher Hitchens. New York: Harper Perennial, 2005, 5–13.

———. "Shakespeare and Religion." In Julian Huxley, *Aldous Huxley*, 163–175.

Secondary Sources

Aldiss, Brian, and David Wingrove. *Trillion Year Spree: The History of Science Fiction.* New York: Atheneum, 1986.

"Aldous Huxley: A Life of the Mind." In Huxley, *Brave New World* and *Brave New World Revisited,* 2–6.

Bedford, Sybille. *Aldous Huxley: A Biography.* New York: Harper & Row, 1974.

Bloom, Harold, ed. *Aldous Huxley's "Brave New World"*. Philadelphia: Chelsea House Publishers, 2003.

Includes contributions from Robert S. Baker, Peter Bowering, June Deery, Peter Edgerly Firchow, William M. Jones, Jerome Meckier, and George Woodcock.

Davis, Daniel F. and Norman Lunger. *A History of the United States Since 1945*. New York: Scholastic, 1987.

Day, Martin A. *History of English Literature: 1837 to the Present*. New York: Doubleday, 1964.

De Koster, Katie, ed. *Readings on "Brave New World"*. San Diego: Greenhaven Press, 1999.

Includes contributions from John Chamberlain, John Clute, Henry Hazlitt, Charles M. Holmes, William Matter, Guinevera A. Nance, Joseph Needham, David W. Sisk, and Donald Watt.

Doyle, Robert P. *Banned Books: 2004 Resource Book*. Chicago, Illinois: American Library Association, 2004.

Dulles, Foster Rhea. *Twentieth Century America*. Boston: Houghton Mifflin, 1945.

Dunaway, David King. *Huxley in Hollywood*. New York: Harper & Row, 1989.

Firchow, Peter. *Aldous Huxley: Satirist and Novelist*. Minneapolis: University of Minnesota Press, 1972.

Fraser, Rebecca. *The Story of Britain: From the Romans to the Present: A Narrative History*. New York: W. W. Norton, 2005.

Freidel, Frank. *America in the Twentieth Century*. New York: Alfred A. Knopf, 1960.

Hitchens, Christopher. "Foreword." *Brave New World* and *Brave New World Revisited*. New York: Harper Perennial, 2005. vii–xxi.

Huxley, Julian, ed. *Aldous Huxley: 1894–1963: A Memorial Volume*. New York: Harper & Row, 1965.
Includes contributions from Isaiah Berlin, David Cecil, T.S. Eliot, Gerald Heard, Robert M. Hutchins, Gervas Huxley, Juliette Huxley, Julian Huxley, Christopher Isherwood, Anita Loos, Raymond Mortimer, Humphry Osmond, Steven Runciman, Osbert Sitwell, Stephen Spender, and Leonard Woolf.

Huxley, Laura Archera. *This Timeless Moment: A Personal View of Aldous Huxley*. Foreword by Terence McKenna. Berkeley, CA: CelestialArts, 2000.

Kateb, George. *Utopia and Its Enemies*. New York: Free Press of Glencoe, 1963.

Kumar, Krishan. *Utopia and Anti-Utopia in Modern Times*. Oxford, UK: Basil Blackwell, 1987.

MacLeish, Archibald. *Actfive and Other Poems*. London: Bodley Head, 1950.

May, Keith M. *Aldous Huxley*. New York: Barnes and Noble Books, 1972.

McKenna, Terence. "Foreword." *This Timeless Moment: A Personal View of Aldous Huxley*, Laura Archera Huxley. Berkeley, CA: CelestialArts, 2000. xi–xv.

Murray, Nicholas. *Aldous Huxley: A Biography*. New York: St. Martin's Press, 2002.

Peck, John and Martin Coyle. *A Brief History of English Literature*. Hampshire, England: Palgrave, 2002.

Sawyer, Dana. *Aldous Huxley: A Biography*. New York: The Crossroad Publishing Company, 2002.

Schrecker, Ellen. *Many Are the Crimes: McCarthyism in America*. Princeton, NJ: Princeton University Press, 1998.

Shakespeare, William. *The Complete Works of William Shakespeare*. Edited by David Bevington. Updated 4th ed. New York: Longman, 1997.

Snowman, Daniel. *America Since 1920*. New York: Harper & Row, 1968.

"Two Far Ahead of Its Time? The Contemporary Response to *Brave New World* (1932)." In Huxley, *Brave New World* and *Brave New World Revisited*, 7–9.

Walsh, Chad. *From Utopia to Nightmare*. New York: Harper & Row, 1962.

Watts, Harold H. *Aldous Huxley*. Boston: Twayne Publishers, 1969.

Sources Using the Words *Brave New World*

Adelman, Kenneth L., and Norman R. Augustine. *Defense Revolution: Strategy for the Brave New World / By an Arms Controller and an Arms Builder*. San Francisco, CA: ICS Press, Institute for Contemporary Studies, 1990.

Anderson, William C. *Roll up the Wallpaper, We're Moving! How to Rip Up Family Roots and Plant Them in a Brave New Green World with Unbelievable Shock to the Nerve Endings and the Pocketbook*. New York: Crown Publishers, 1970.

Beck, Ulrich. *Brave New World of Work*. Translated by Patrick Camiller. Malden, MA: Polity Press, 2000.

Brave New World?: Living with Information Technology. New York: Pergamorn Press, 1983.

Brave New World of Medical Malpractice Litigation. Mechanicsburg, PA: Pennsylvania Bar Institute, 2008.

Brave New World of Oil Prices: A Permanent Shift Upward? Cambridge, MA: CERA, 2004.

Brave New World: Where Biotechnology and Human Rights Intersect. [Ottawa]: Government of Canada, 2005.

Bredvold, Louis I. *Brave New World of the Enlightenment*. Ann Arbor: University of Michigan Press, 1961.

Carlson, Rick J., and Gary Stimeling. *Terrible Gift: The Brave New World of Genetic Medicine*. New York: PublicAffairs, 2002.

Cheru, Fantu. *Not So Brave New World!: Problems and Prospects of Regional Integrations in Post Apartheid Southern Africa*. Johannesburg: South African Institute of International Affairs, 1992.

Cooke, Robert. *Improving on Nature: The Brave New World of Genetic Engineering*. New York: Quadrangle/The New York Times Book Co., 1977.

Dahl, Francis W. *Dahl's Brave New World*. Cartoons by Francis W. Dahl. Text by Charles W. Morton. Boston: Little, Brown, 1947.

Day, David, ed. *Brave New World: Dr. H. V. Evatt and Australian Foreign Policy, 1941–1949*. Portland, OR: International Specialized Book Services, 1996.

De Menta, Boye. *Eros' Revenge: The Brave New World of American Sex*. Phoenix, AR: Phoenix Books, 1979.

De Mingo, Kaminouchi Alberto, Celia Deane-Drummond, and Ted Peters. *Brave New World?: Theology, Ethics, and the Human Genome*. Foreword by Ted Peters. New York: T & T Clark International, 2003.

Duffy, Helen, and Frances K. Smith. *Brave New World of Fritz Brandtner / Le Meilleur des Mondes de Fritz Brandtner*. Kingston, Ontario, Canada: Agnes Etherington Art Centre, Queen's University, 1982.

Edmunds, John C. *Brave New Wealthy World: Winning the Struggle for World Prosperity*. Upper Saddle River, NJ: Prentice Hall, 2003.

Eisenach, Jeffrey August. *America's Fiscal Future 1991: The Federal Budget's Brave New World*. Indianapolis, IN: Hudson Institute, 1991.

Feinberg, John S., and Paul D. Feinberg. *Ethics for a Brave New World*. Wheaton, IL: Crossway Books, 1993.

Fjermedal, Grant. *Tomorrow Makers: A Brave New World of Living-Brain Machines*. New York: Macmillan, 1986. Reprinted: Redmond, WA: Tempus Books of Microsoft Press, 1988.

Fox, Michael W. *Superpigs and Wondercorn: The Brave New World of Biotechnology and Where It All May Lead*. New York: Lyons and Burford, 1992.

Gosden, R. G. *Designing Babies: The Brave New World of Reproductive Technology*. New York: W. H. Freeman, 1999.

Gibbon, Peter. *Limping Towards a Ditch Without a Crutch: The Brave New World of Tanzanian Cotton Marketing Cooperatives*. Copenhagen, Denmark: Centre for Development Research, 1998.

Golder, John, and Richard Madelaine, eds. *O Brave New World: Two Centuries of Shakespeare on the Australian Stage*. Sydney, Australia: Currency Press, 2001.

Gueutal, Hal G., and Dianna L. Stone, eds. *Brave New World of eHR: Human Resources Management in the Digital Age*. San Francisco: Jossey-Bass, 2005.

Halpern, Paul, and Paul Wesson. *Brave New Universe: Illuminating the Darkest Secrets of the Cosmos*. Washington, DC: Joseph Henry Press, 2006.

Healthcare Joint Ventures: The Brave New World. Harrisburg, PA: Pennsylvania Bar Institute, 1993.

Herbergs, Johannes. *Brave New World: Rhinelanders Conquer America: The Journal of Johannes Herbergs*. Ed. by Dieter Pesch. Trans. by Angelika and David Orpin. [Nümbrecht, Germany]: Galunder, 2001.

Ho, Mae-Wan. *Genetic Engineering, Dream or Nightmare?: Turning the Tide on the Brave New World of Bad Science and Big Business*. New York: Continuum, 2000.

Hoffer, Peter Charles. *Brave New World: A History of Early America*. Boston: Houghton Mifflin, 2000. Reprinted. Baltimore: Johns Hopkins University Press, 2006.

Hyde, Margaret O., and John F. Setaro. *Medicine's Brave New World: Bioengineering and the New Genetics*. Brookfield, CT: Twenty-First Century Books, 2001.

ITA Organization. *Agenda for Change: The Brave New World of Digital: Proceedings / ITA Twenty-Third Annual Seminar*, Phoenix, Arizona, March 10–14, 1993. New York: ITA, 1993.

Lamm, Richard D. *Brave New World of Health Care*. Golden, CO: Fulcrum Pubublications, 2003.

Lightman, Alex with William Rojas. *Brave New Unwired World: The Digital Big Bang and the Infinite Internet*. New York: J. Wiley & Sons, 2002.

Martin, Andres, and George Ross, et al. *Brave New World of European Labor: European Trade Unions at the Millennium*. New York: Berghahn Press, 1999.

McCormick, Richard A. *How Brave a New World?: Dilemmas in Bioethics*. Washington, DC: Georgetown University Press, 1981.

McDonagh, Bobby. *Original Sin in a Brave New World: The Paradox of Europe: An Account of the Negotiation of the Treaty of Amsterdam*. Foreword by Jacques Santer. Dublin: Institute of European Affairs, 1998.

Mead, Sidney Earl. *Old Religion in the Brave New World: Reflections on the Relation Between Christendom and the Republic*. Berkeley: University of California Press, 1977.

Miller, Donald N. *My Son, My Son: One Man's Arduous Journey from the Old Country to a Brave New World*. Hillsboro, OR: D. N. Miller, 1997.

Nearing, Helen, and Scott Nearing. *Brave New World.* Harborside, ME: Social Science Institute, 1958.

Nelson-Pallmeyer, Jack. *Brave New World Order: Must We Pledge Allegiance?* Maryknoll, NY: Orbis Books, 1992.

Pinnix, John L., ed. *Ethics in a Brave New World: Professional Responsibility, Personal Accountability, and Risk Management for Immigration Practitioners.* Washington, DC: American Immigration Lawyers Association, 2004.

Pleszczynski, Wladyslaw, ed. *Our Brave New World: Essays on the Impact of September 11.* Stanford, CA: Hoover Institution Press, 2002.

Preeg, Ernest H. *Traders in a Brave New World: The Uruguay Round and the Future of the International Trading System.* Chicago: University of Chicago Press, 1995.

Rosenblatt, Seymour, and Reynolds Dodson. *Beyond Valium: The Brave New World of Psychochemistry.* New York: Putnam, 1981.

Salter, Leonard M. *Law as a Lever: Building a Brave New World.* New York: Vantage Press, 1987.

Schaller, Barry R. *Understanding Bioethics and the Law: The Promises and Perils of the Brave New World of Biotechnology.* Foreword by Todd Brewster. Westport, CT: Praeger, 2008.

Schappert, Phillip Joseph. *Last Monarch Butterfly: Conserving the Monarch Butterfly in a Brave New World.* Buffalo, NY: Firefly Books, 2004.

Sherk, Bill. *More Brave New Words: The Latest, Funniest, and Most Original Dictionary in the World*. Illustrations by Leah Taylor. Garden City, NY: Doubleday, 1981.

Silver, Lee M. *Remaking Eden: Cloning and Beyond in a Brave New World*. New York: Avon Books, 1997.

Smith, George Patrick, II. *Bioethics and the Law: Medical, Socio-Legal and Philosophical Directions for a Brave New World*. Lanham, MD: University Press of America, 1993.

Stewart, Susan D. *Brave New Stepfamilies: Diverse Paths Toward Stepfamily Living*. Thousand Oaks, CA: Sage Publications, 2007.

Tada, Joni Eareckson, and Nigel M. de S. Cameron. *How to be a Christian in a Brave New World*. Grand Rapids, MI: Zondervan, 2006.

Tan, Chung. *China and the Brave New World: A Study of the Origins of the Opium War*. Durham, NC: Carolina Academic Press, 1978.

Thompson, Matthew C., and Caroline A. Raufi. *Brave New World, Reloaded, Unraveling the Digital Matrix: The 28th Annual UCLA Entertainment Law Symposium*. [Los Angeles], CA: Regents of the University of California, 2004.

Utagawa, Reiz. *Brave New World: Can Japanese Domestic Politics Change?* Tokyo, Japan: International Institute for Global Peace, 1992.

Wasserstrom, Jeffrey N. *China's Brave New World–And Other Tales for Global Times*. Foreword by Vladimir Tismaneanu. Bloomington, IN: Indiana University Press, 2007.

Weeramantry, C. G. *Armageddon, or, Brave New World?: Reflections on the Hostilities in Iraq*. Colombo, Sri Lanka: Weeramantry International Centre for Peace, Education & Research, 2003.

West, Julian. *Just Another Brave New World? Oil Companies and Iraq*. Cambridge, MA: CERA, 2003.

Index

Page numbers in **boldface** are illustrations, tables, and charts.
Proper names of fictional characters are shown by (C).

About the Author

Raychel Haugrud Reiff, a professor of English at the University of Wisconsin-Superior, has published seven books in Marshall Cavendish Benchmark's Writers and Their Works series, as well as numerous articles on literary topics. Her most recent book in this series is *William Golding: "Lord of the Flies."* She lives in Superior, Wisconsin.